THIS ABOVE ALL

A Journey of Self-Discovery

Tess Hughes

TAT Foundation Press

Published by TAT Foundation Press
47 Washington Avenue #150
Wheeling, West Virginia 26003
www.tatfoundation.org

Text font: Minion Pro

Main entry under title: *This Above All: A Journey of Self-Discov-ery*

1. Spirituality   2. Psychology

ISBN: 978-0-9864457-1-2

Library of Congress Control Number: 2015960839

Interior photos: Bob Fergeson of nostalgiawest.com – pp. 122
and 136. Tess Hughes – All other photos (Croagh Patrick, Co.
Mayo, Ireland. It has been a pilgrimage site since pre-Christian
times. The author grew up in its shadow.)

Cover design: Bob Fergeson – Author photo by Marc Pruss –
Front cover: Croagh Patrick – Back cover: Beach on Inis Oirr,
Co. Galway, Ireland

This book is dedicated to Manus and Sabina, the lights of my life.

Contents

Prologue

A few years ago a man wrote asking me if I would consider writing my biography, focusing on my spiritual journey. At the time I said no and couldn't imagine ever doing such a thing, but here I am having done it. It happened spontaneously and effortlessly.

One day I came across a booklet I had in my house and didn't remember ever having seen it. It was Bernadette Roberts' "A Christian Commentary on The Ten Ox-Herding Pictures." What are the Ox-Herding Pictures? Here's how John Daido Loori, Abbot of The Zen Mountain Monastery in Mount Tremper, New York, describes them in his book: *Riding the Ox Home: (Stages on the Path of Enlightenment)* by Shambhala Publications.

> In my days of Zen study, I and all the other students really wanted to have a sense of what we had accomplished and the challenges to come. For these reasons we have created at Zen Mountain Monastery a somewhat arbitrary but helpful map of training, based on a series of paintings from Chinese antiquity known as The Ox-Herding Pictures. They illustrate the spiritual development of a student, from the moment they begin their spiritual quest until the completion of their training, when they become a teacher in their own right.

The following quote taken from the back cover of the same book gives a further description of the value of *The Ox-Herding Pictures.*

> Maps and guideposts are helpful when we undertake a journey. The ten ox-herding pictures, the accompanying ancient poems, and a modern commentary by John Daido Loori sketch the spiritual path encountered in Zen training, a path of exhaustive study of the self and the realization of the ultimate nature of Reality. The Ox-Herding Pictures can be our companion on the Way of self-discovery, our compass and perspective when we need one. They are a bottomless source of mysterious wisdom to which we can return again and again for inspiration, and they translate easily into the gritty reality of spiritual practice that emerges out of and grounds us in the inescapable relevance of our daily lives.

I knew them—*The Ox-Herding Pictures*—but hadn't studied them much. However, I see this book as echoing the "gritty reality" and the "inescapable relevance of our daily lives." That is what this book is about.

There are many versions of the stages and maps of the spiritual path. Teresa of Avila describes these stages as seven mansions, inner mansions. Many others have described stages ranging from as few as three or four to as many as fifteen recognizable stages. *A Course in Miracles* describes the path in six stages. The traditional Christian path describes three phases:

1-Purgative, 2 - Illuminative, and 3- Unitive. John of The Cross describes it as Four Nights of the Soul: Active and Passive Nights of the Senses and Active and Passive Nights of the Spirit (Soul). And all the other traditions have their own maps. But the thing to remember is that "the map is not the territory," as Alfred Korzybski said. There are many maps for this journey each using their own mythological language to describe it.

The fact that these maps exist is in itself encouraging in that they document the possibility inherent in the human condition. But, it is important to remember and act on what Lao Tzu says in the *Tao Te Ching*: "Every journey begins with a single step." We all have to take our own steps, as the opening lines of The Tao say:

> The Way that can be told of
> is not an unvarying way;
>
> The names that can be named
> are not unvarying names.
>
> It was from the Nameless
> that Heaven and Earth sprang;
>
> The named is but the mother that rears the ten
> thousand creatures, each after its kind.

On reading Roberts' booklet, concerning the Ox-Herding Pictures, I could identify five or six of the stages described, and I could precisely name the event or experience that had been a milestone or transition from one stage to the next. I had never been able to do this while on the path, but now, four years after the end of seeking, I could recognize stages I had passed

9

through. So, I started to write descriptions of the stages I recognized. Over the coming days the stages I hadn't recognized became apparent. In about two weeks, the whole path had been written as it happened in my personal experience.

Every version of the spiritual journey is but a particular version of a universal process. However, while going through it I could not ever identify where I was on the path. I couldn't distinguish between the various stages in anything I read. But, I did know and was comforted and inspired by writings documenting the stages of possible evolution for an individual. The very idea of this possibility made it too much to ignore. Therefore to aid my journey, I deliberately sought out books written by women in the hopes that I might better relate to or understand what this path might look like for a woman. And this did help. The way women wrote made the possibility seem more accessible for me. Having said that, most of my reading and inspiration came from men, including the person I call my teacher, Art Ticknor. However, at the end of the day, spiritual evolution is beyond gender. It is about the human condition and we are all in the same boat: cut off from our True Selves.

The effortlessness with which this book came out is surprising, but then I am writing about my own experience and don't have to think much about it in order to access it. My reason for writing it, or publishing it, is in an effort to communicate what I think is the most significant knowledge that can be put in the hands of another person. It is my (effortless) effort to contribute something to the store of perennial wisdom of the world, which is what inspired me to follow this path. The Perennial Wisdom is available in all cultures at all times, constantly being renewed and re-articulated in the language of the day by those who have come to the end of seeking.

I read a lot, for decades, and cannot name most of the books I read now, but this constant reading led to a slow accumulation of ideas and practices that eventually prepared me for conscious seeking. It prepared me so that I recognized real spiritual teaching when I came across it. My hope in writing this is that you, the reader, will be inspired to actively follow your path. Your path and your experiences will not look like mine, but after it's over, you too will see that your life was not a random series of experiences but that it was always moving towards a particular goal; it was always trying to return you to your natural state, your Home. It's a question of you becoming aware of what is really going on in your life and then doing what you can to align your life with your innermost Self or God's will.

At the end of the day, this is all about coming to the end of suffering, the healing of our existential angst, which is the root cause of all our suffering: our anxiety, our insecurities, our lack of love, our lack of self-acceptance. It's about coming to know our true identity, our identity beyond that of being a creature of the world. This possibility exists for everyone, but we have to work for it. The work we have to do is to be willing to look deep into our own minds and emotions and experiences and see what is really going on. The Dali Lama says "Happiness is not something ready-made. It comes from your own actions." We have to take responsibility for our own lives; that's the first step. Nobody else is to blame, no matter how attached we are to such a story.

I think that for many people the notion of taking full responsibility for their own state of happiness or maturity or spiritual development is a foreign idea. However, spiritual progress relies on each of us taking full responsibility for our own fruition into the full potential inherent in the human condition, as each of us experience it. Our relationship with ourselves is the most important relationship we will ever have. We die alone. Nobody else can accompany us on that journey.

Our first reaction to this statement might be that this is selfish. Many people have said this to me, but I can assure you that the opposite is true. Having a good relationship with yourself, knowing who you really are is the greatest gift you can give to others. Remember though, paying attention to yourself, your inner world, in no way means that you neglect your relationship with others. But giving all your energy and attention to others at the expense of your relationship with yourself is refusing to take on the potential inherent in your life. It's unlikely that others will encourage you to do this, but then they are not suffering your suffering.

Nobody has the right to prevent us from healing our inner wound and we need to know this in order to have the confidence to follow our path. People may not understand what we are doing and so be inclined to dismiss it. We don't have to have anyone else's permission to do what is necessary to heal our suffering, and we can do it right in the middle of ordinary life. I did. I did it by retaining some of my energy and time for this inner work, and at the same time I honored all my responsibilities to others in my life. They didn't even notice what I was doing really. This inner journey is private and can be done while washing the dishes or walking to the shop. Everyone can carve out time for it once they see the need for it. Admittedly, there are phases in life when we may be overrun by responsibilities, as for instance when we are raising a family and working outside of the home. But, even then, to neglect our relationship with ourselves completely is asking for trouble.

It's not a question of time; it's a question of understanding that the goal of spiritual development is finding peace within. Looking back on my journey, the main part of it took place over the course of my life, but the intense part took about five years. For three years before the final revelation, it had come to dominate my life. My inner life had come to the fore with daily life in the background, and my attention was directed towards the inner changes that were taking place. It had become an obsession. In addition, this coincided with menopause, which is commonly referred to as The Change. I have to wonder if this period in a woman's life is not more conducive to spiritual growth than any other.

As I say in the book, I had many physical symptoms going on and when I Googled them, I always got back both menopause and kundalini. I couldn't distinguish between these symptoms, but the kundalini symptoms stopped completely following the revelation, end of seeking, and the menopause symptoms continued. So, now I can see how they were different. For one thing menopause symptoms are more dense and general in the body. The kundalini symptoms moved up the body, starting in the pelvic area and finishing in the head, and then vanished. I don't have any explanation for these physical symptoms. I haven't read much about Kundalini. I took the attitude that they were another aspect of the inner change that was happening and not the primary thing. In other words, I

13

didn't get hung up on the symptoms, which I think is a problem that many get lost in.

For two years after the revelation, I found it difficult to participate in daily life other than in a minimal way, but that has changed, and I am now able to participate fully again. So, I'd say, the intense part of the spiritual path took five years. John Moriarty, an Irish writer, refers to this intense phase of spiritual unfolding as The Tridium Sacrum and wonders if we'll ever see the day when people can take time off work to undergo their "tridium sacrum" in much the same way as maternity leave is given now to have a baby.

This book is written in the spirit of sharing "spiritual labor" because it is difficult enough to find such information, and yet it is a universal phenomenon. I grew up in a culture and time where the physical labor of birthing a baby was not talked about. So I went into my own first labor with little more than trust that it would work out fine. It would have been helpful, I think, to have had a better idea of what to expect. However, having said that, "labor" does its thing whether we understand it, or are prepared for it, or not. Knowing about such things in no way alleviates us of the need to live through it. I recognized that I was going through a spiritual process, or as I called it "a spiritual pregnancy," for about three years and knew that this would one day lead to a birthing, but I had no idea what that might entail. Actually I don't think anyone can be prepared for this event other than knowing that this is what is happening, in both the spiritual and biological sense.

The book has ten main chapters, based on the traditional ox-herding story from the Zen Buddhist tradition. The version of the poem used is taken from a course given by Dr. John M. Koller, Department of Cognitive Science, Rensselaer Polytechnic Institute. Dr. Koller credits the version he uses as such:

> The twelfth century monk Guo-an Shi-yuan (also known as Kuo-an Shih-yuan or Kakuan Shien) revised and expanded upon the traditional Taoist story of the ox and the oxherd by creating a series of ten images and accompanying verses to simultaneously depict and narrate this well-known tale. Guo-an's version subsequently became one of the most popular and enduring versions of the parable. Nevertheless, despite the dominance of Guo-an's paintings, other Zen Buddhists and artists have repeatedly repainted and retranslated Guo-an's immortal verses throughout the following centuries. While the illustrations of the tale vary, the verses tend to be either direct or indirect translations of Guo-an's original verses, and their message stands unchanged.

Each chapter begins with a verse of the Ox-herding poem and is followed by the explanation, in italics, given by Dr. John Koller. Each chapter finishes with a Bernadette Roberts commentary on the ox-herding verse from a Christian perspective.

This is my personal journey home to the source, and I have shaped it along the milestones taught in the Zen Buddhist tradition, as depicted in the well-known ox-herding pictures. While this journey of inner transformation is a universal process, it plays out and is experienced in a uniquely personal way for each one. This book is but one person's story or description of this universal process of inner transformation, which is usually referred to as the spiritual journey or path.

So, I hope you find inspiration and ideas in the following pages to help you on your way, on your great journey Home.

THE SEARCH BEGINS

1. The Search for the Ox

In the pasture of the world,
I endlessly push aside the tall
grasses in search of the ox.
Following unnamed rivers,
lost upon the interpenetrating
paths of distant mountains,
My strength failing and my vitality
exhausted, I cannot find the ox.
I only hear the locusts chirping
through the forest at night.

The first picture shows the oxherd desperately looking everywhere for his lost ox. He is dissatisfied with his life, unable to find the true happiness that he seeks. His efforts to secure wealth, friends, fame, and pleasure have not brought him the fulfilment he is seeking. Like many of us, he is seeking something, though he is not sure exactly what it is that will make life meaningful and bring him lasting happiness. (John Koller)

I grew up in medieval times—well not really! But, living on a small farm in the West of Ireland in the 1950's, we drew water from the well, we milked our cows by hand, we cut and saved turf for our fires, we tilled our land with horse-drawn ploughs, and we cooked on an open fire and went barefoot in summer. Maybe this is why I could relate to the story of the ox-herding boy of far away and long ago as a metaphor for life, the journey we are all on. It took me a long time to realize that the ox in the story is a metaphor for wisdom. It's the story of the stages or milestones we meet along the path to the realization of our True Nature—Wisdom. Wisdom is a natural attraction for humans. We are all seeking it. It is how all religions started out. It has been found by countless people across all cultures and eras.

However, knowing or understanding the story is only the beginning because the path to wisdom is not a path of knowing but of transformation, of becoming what/who we already are. It is nothing less than a transmutation from what we think or believe we are to what we truly are.

How does my story begin, you might ask? I don't know for others, but for myself I can trace it back to childhood, as I suspect many on this path can. There was the wonderment of the universe, the sense of magic at being part of this something awesome. How did it all happen? How did it begin? Where was I before you got me, Mammy? How did I get to be me? I cannot imagine a child who hasn't had some moments of sheer wonder at it all. But, then we lose it.

One beautiful summer's morning when I was around six or seven, I was in the field across the road from our house, doing something like picking flowers with my sisters or trying to spot rabbits or frogs, when I stood staring at the sky and clouds and everything, quivering with excitement at the enormity of it all and the wonder of it all. I had the thought, "I wonder why everyone isn't always staring at this 'amazement' unable to drag themselves from it." Then I saw my father rushing from the barns to the house, obviously in a hurry. Something urgent was happening. Then the thought arose, "I have to stop this 'staring' or I won't be able to grow up and do the work—the work of being a responsible adult in the world." And I was well aware that my existence depended on having responsible parents.

At the time I didn't think anything of this experience, nor would I have had the words to say anything about it, but something of the sense of that wonderment never quite left me. It was as if I always knew that there was something more behind everyday life, and I would get around to finding or understanding it one day. I was sure that all the adults around me knew about it and that it was only a matter of growing up and I too would be in on the secret. It didn't happen that way. It doesn't happen that way for anyone!

By the time I was a teenager, and we didn't have that word in those days, I was a full-time boarding student in an all-girls Catholic school. Books, literature, poetry were my great loves. They kept me sane and allowed me to see that these writers were writing about the mystery, or the really important things in life. I got into classic western literature: Shakespeare, Milton, Yeats, Tolstoy, Kafka, Virginia Woolf, and others. I got the idea that there was a big picture to life, and I wanted it. I knew there was more to life than a career and the accumulation of wealth; there was the possibility of becoming a person of integrity.

I didn't know what I meant by integrity in those days, but from my reading and from observation of those around me, I knew that it was possible for a person to grow in integrity or develop character, and that this required some input from the individual. I could also see that being religious was no guarantee of becoming a person of character or integrity. With hindsight it is interesting how apt this word was: integrity having two definitions in the dictionary: one, the quality of being honest and having strong moral principles, and two, the state of being whole and undivided.

Throughout this time I was also hearing sermons on Christian teachings. I didn't make the connection between these teachings and becoming a person of integrity, but I did have a religious or devotional feeling. I was also reading romantic novels and anything I could get my hands on. One thing I am grateful for that we did in this school was to have a retreat every year. The retreat involved three days spent in silence, listening to talks by a priest whose work was to give retreats to teenagers, while we read spiritual literature. During one of those retreats the priest ended one of his stories with the statement: "The secret of life is to act—not to react." "Great!" I thought. "I have found what I had been looking for: the secret of life."

The following day I got in some trouble with the principal for some minor incident I have long since forgotten. I decided to "act" and not "react" by telling her my side of the story. She was shocked at the change that had come over me and said I had become a very cheeky and insolent girl. Since I didn't have any practice in being called such names, I decided I better give up on the "acting" thing in school. During another one of those retreats I had taken a book, *The Interior Castle* by Teresa of Avila, as my chosen reading. When one nun saw what I was reading, she said it was not suitable reading for me and replaced it with something like the life of a martyr. But, I made the intention that I would get this book as soon as I could to see what I was not supposed to be reading. I had chosen it because it was written by the saint after whom I had been named. I had the idea that I should learn to be like my name giver, learn to be a true Teresa.

Shakespeare was my great love. We studied a few of his plays in detail and I was just in awe of anyone having such an

1. The Search for the Ox

understanding of human life, even if he had lived 400 years before me. I remember the day we read and discussed the lines in Hamlet: Polonius' advice to Laertes:

> This above all—to thine own self be true,
> And it must follow, as the night the day,
> Thou canst not then be false to any man.

I knew I wasn't true to myself, but I thought this was my peculiar condition and Shakespeare had named it. I had a diagnosis. The question now was: how do I correct it?

Shortly afterwards I was home for the holidays. I was wondering how I could try out being true to myself in circumstances that didn't leave much room for individual variation. I had always liked carrots but couldn't think of any other way of trying out being true to myself other than announcing that I didn't like carrots anymore, having left them behind on my dinner plate one day. When I didn't eat my carrots at dinner my mother asked why and I said I didn't like carrots anymore.

The following day she served carrots and cabbage with the dinner. We usually only had one vegetable with dinner and I asked her why two today. She said it was because I no longer ate carrots and I needed to have a vegetable every day. I was upset and ate my carrots. I was upset because my efforts at being true to myself caused my mother extra work. Another failed experiment!

I figured out that I couldn't be true to myself at the expense of others. My notion about being a person of integrity included not causing trouble or extra work for others. While I didn't have a clear idea of what I meant by integrity, I knew when something went against it. This was how I interpreted a conscience. Funny that I should remember these little experiments all these years later, when I remember so little else from my teenage and school years. I see this as my first efforts at "searching for the ox."

I went to University when I was eighteen. I picked almost at random what to study and it turned out to be science. Because of my love of literature, I felt sure I would always read but felt that science was an area that I needed some help with. I also felt it might "contain" the answer to what life was about. Studying science did change things for me. I soon realized that science didn't hold the answers to the big questions in life, which was my main interest.

Science, however, gave me a new perspective on the Catholic Church. Despite having grown up in a religious household and having attended a Catholic school, I was unable to make sense of much of what I heard and had become aware of, like misogyny, in the Catholic Church. The atheistic view that was in vogue amongst my fellow science students swayed me totally away from incomprehensible beliefs of the Catholic Church. But, this posed a very painful situation for me. I had to become dishonest with my parents – pretending that I was practicing my religion while away at college. I went through several years of real anguish about my loss of faith, and this deception, and while I had all the arguments for atheism, I was disappointed by it. It was a big letdown in comparison to the possibility of eternal life. I was really disappointed and upset by the loss of wisdom teachings that would guide me through life. I felt the need for guidance but couldn't see it in what was offered to me in the Catholic teachings or science or atheism.

However, sex and drugs and rock-and-roll, so to speak, took over most of my attention at this time. By this I mean, I had a boyfriend, I partied, as students tend to do, and I enjoyed all the things young people do. I loved fashionable clothes. I got opportunities to travel... I was not a studious student!

This phase of my life came to a rather sudden end because I got married the week I finished college to a man in my class whom I had met the first month in college. Ten years later we broke up painfully with two children to be reared. By now a new genre of reading had entered my life—self-help books. I bought and absorbed every one that I heard about. I was suffering. This is not what I had anticipated in my life. I was trying to fix myself of some un-nameable discontent. And it wasn't working. I was isolated. I had nobody to talk to about this problem. We didn't talk about our problems in those days (in Ireland), at least that was the very definite message I got from anyone I broached the subject with. Or else, I was asked what had I to complain about— didn't I have it all? And I had to agree, on the surface I had, but this forced sense of isolation on top of the problems I was experiencing led me to believe that there was something fundamentally wrong with me to be feeling this way and that this was not normal. The fundamental sense of abandonment and separation I was experiencing at the time I later came to recognize as existential angst, but at that time I was still trying to heal it by worldly means.

There were a few self-help books I remember that had a long lasting effect on me. One was *Passages*, by Gail Sheehy, which I read while in hospital giving birth to my second child. In this book Gail lays out the various passages that we go through in adult life, based on research she had done. I've seen a summary of the passages as; The Trying Twenties, The Catch Thirties, The Forlorn Forties, The Refreshed (Resigned) Fifties.

Sheehy's book is about the passages, the universal stages of psychological growth, that we all go through, if they don't get aborted or deflected along the way. The intention of this book is to describe this universal human journey, going beyond the psychological realm into the spiritual realm through one particular story. It's just one variation on a universal theme as is each one's journey. The ox-herding pictures are another version of passages, from the spiritual perspective. It's a much bigger picture.

At twenty seven when I read Sheehy's book, I didn't really apply the passages to myself. At twenty seven it is hard to imagine what being forty might be like. I did, however, pick up on the notion that each life crises is an opportunity for further growth in the direction of becoming a person of integrity or developing character. While going through the various crises, I didn't usually remember this notion, but with hindsight I can say that this is true. We can resist growth by denying or refusing to make the required changes to our lifestyle and attitude to life. Or we can accept the new circumstances as they arise and do what we can to adjust to them. I was so unwilling to accept that my marriage was not going according to "my plan" that I went very far down the road of denial, despite having the idea of passages to be lived through, and that this was how growth happened. Intellectual knowledge is one thing— living it is another thing altogether.

Erik Erikson's model for human psychosocial development, in his book *Identity and Life Cycle*, describes this stage of

26

adult development as the conflict between intimacy and isolation and he designates it as "Early Adulthood." He believed that a strong sense of personal identity was necessary in order for an individual to form a committed secure loving relationship. He says, "Studies have demonstrated that those with a poor sense of self tend to have less committed relationships and are more likely to suffer emotional isolation, loneliness, and depression."

I had a poor sense of self. I defined myself in relation to others, especially in my roles as wife and mother. I had no idea who I was in myself. I didn't recognize or admit to myself that I had needs. The conditioning of woman as a set of roles in society was what I operated from. My feeling at the time was that I had a lot of responsibilities but no rights. I wouldn't have been able to articulate this, but it was the feeling and attitude I had about myself. It's no wonder I felt "isolated, lonely and depressed." I suspect that many people, both men and women go through this at some stage in their lives. In the absence of having a wisdom tradition or guidance for life available to them, they remain stuck or turn to the various therapies and psychiatry. Therapies of all kinds are a great help in getting through the crises and having a wisdom tradition to lean on does not alleviate us of having to go through these crises.

My crisis became so intense that I nearly committed suicide. We were married about eight years and the children were about four and six at this time. I had it all planned, razor blades, on the wrists and jugular vein, in a bath of warm water. I had gradually sunk into a place where the thought and planning of this were the only comfort I had. I did love my two small children beyond words but somehow my distress was so great that I had lost my ability to make a real judgement about what I was planning. And, I had no one to talk to about this. I was all set to do it one afternoon, while my children were at the nursery and were to be picked up by their father. However, as I was about to do it, an image appeared before my eyes showing me the look on my children's faces when they ran into the bathroom all excited to see me and found instead a bath-full of blood and a dead Mammy.

I got out of the bath, got rid of the blades and made a commitment that I would never do such a thing for the sake of my beloved children. And with that, I got the energy or determination to start making a plan, a plan to leave the marriage. It was what Virginia Woolf called a "moment of being," a moment when a different light shines through on our mundane life, bringing with it an impulse towards change. According to Sheehy, this is how the next developmental stage begins.

One of the things that makes it difficult to recognize when a stage has started and finished is that there is usually a period, maybe months or years during which we are between clearly recognizable stages. During this period, incidents and events can look like they are random and it is not obvious that they are going in a particular direction. It's only with hindsight that we can see the direction that was developing.

God is looking for us. He wants us. We may not know it, but we belong to Him. He even hunts us down to be sure we know it. Though we may hear His voice calling, even see Him from afar, we keep going our own way. Still, He follows relentlessly – and we know we are being tailed. He must want something from us, but

1. The Search for the Ox

what could that be? What can anyone possibly give God? (Berna-dette Roberts – Looking for the Ox)

Noticing the Footprints

2. Noticing the Footprints

Along the riverbank under the trees,
I discover footprints.
Even under the fragrant grass,
I see his prints.
Deep in remote mountains they are found.
These traces can no more be hidden
than one's nose, looking heavenward.

The second picture shows that the oxherd has now caught sight of the tracks of the ox, bringing hope that his ox is not lost forever. This could be interpreted to mean that he has recognized his distress and has begun to seek for a solution in the teachings of Buddhism or in other teachings. But he is still at the stage of thinking and talking about his problems and various possible solutions. He has not yet found a path to follow and has not yet started to practice. (John Koller)

One of the qualities of integrity is courage, having the courage of one's convictions. Well, I didn't have courage. I had desperation. After my marriage broke up, people often commented on what a courageous move that had been. I didn't feel that it was courageous, but in its wake hope and confidence began to develop. It was my first experience that things can and do work out after a crisis. It was the beginnings of trust in self-reliance. The doorway to becoming a mature adult had opened.

In the last few years prior to the breakup of the marriage, looking to ease my discontent, I had been reading all kinds of self-help books, and I had come across a small second-hand book shop in Dublin which dealt in occult books and goods. I had gone in a few times, bought an I-Ching, Tarot cards, and some items such as crystals. One day the man behind the higgledy-piggledy stack of exotic items and tatty books asked if he could suggest a book that he thought would be of interest to me. I bought it. It was Jiddu Krishnamurti's *The First and the Last Freedom.* I immediately recognized it as being of a different quality to my usual self-help and psychology oriented reading. By now I had given up on classical literature because my need was much more immediate than intellectual discussions about the great conflicts of life. I was reading it a page or paragraph at a time and trying to take it in. I had gotten about halfway through it when it disappeared and to this day I do not know what happened to it. However, noticing the footprints, looking for the ox, had begun—although I did not know this at the time.

What struck me about this book was the clarity of the writing and the topics being discussed. He was asking much bigger questions than found in self-help books. He was addressing the radical questions that had interested me so much as a teenager, but that I had forgotten about in the meantime.

Below is a quote, by J. Krishnamurti, found in the second chapter of *The First and The Last Freedom* entitled, "What Are We Seeking?":

> So we have to come to the point when we ask ourselves, really earnestly and profoundly, if peace, happiness, reality, God, or what you will, can be given to us by someone else. Can this incessant search, this longing, give us that extraor-

dinary sense of reality, that creative being, which comes when we really understand ourselves? Does self-knowledge come through search, through following someone else, through be- longing to any particular organization, through reading books, and so on? After all, that is the main issue, is it not?, that so long as I do not understand myself, I have no basis for thought, and all my search will be in vain. I can escape into illusions; I can run away from contention, strife, struggle; I can worship another; I can look for my salvation through somebody else. But so long as I am ignorant of myself, so long as I am unaware of the total process of myself I have no basis for thought, for affection, for action.

Coming across this book led to a shift in the kind of reading material I sought out and activities I engaged in.

In the spring of 1978, I remember the day well since Dublin was covered in snow and this was unusual, I was initi- ated into TM—The Transcendental Meditation movement that was enjoying popularity at the time. I remember the day because of the snow, the purity and the silence everywhere around. My children were but babies at the time, and I asked my husband to mind them for a couple of hours while I did something for myself. He did it but it was by way of a big favor. This was the nature of our relationship. He did not approve of the "gobbledygook" I was getting into. He found it embarrass- ing and did not want me to mention it to anyone. Despite his resistance I felt very drawn to explore TM and had high hopes that it would alleviate my discontent.

This was my first introduction to meditation and it had a startling effect on me, especially when we had a group meditation. My hearing became very clear. Every time I meditated with my mantra my hearing became really clear. I enjoyed this, so I did my best to keep up my two twenty minute sessions per day as advised, but it proved impossible. Between having a full time job as a teacher and the children, I simply couldn't find the time to do it on most days. Even when I did find the necessary twenty minutes to go to my bedroom in order to do my meditation, the children cried for me or played outside the door, peeking in regularly to see what I was up to.

A few weeks after I was initiated I met the man who had initiated me into the TM, and he asked me how I was getting on with my practice. I told him that I couldn't find one twenty minute meditation period in the day, let alone two, but that I loved it when I did it. He said "If you cannot find twenty minutes in the day for yourself, you need to look at your lifestyle." He had hit on my sorest nerve. I knew I was going under from working a full-time job, and being a full-time mother and housekeeper, but I couldn't see any way to change any bit of it. It was about four years later when the day in the bath happened. I suspect that many women do not realize the problems that are building up for them by neglecting to have time for themselves. I certainly thought I was managing at the time, and I was living in the hope of things easing off before too long. I didn't realize that I had taken on too much and that my life was unsustainable. Something had to give.

Some months after the marriage broke up, and the kids were spending some time with their father, a friend suggested that I might like to investigate a spiritual group in Dublin. It turned out to be a Fourth Way School, based on the teachings of George Gurdjieff. I went to the talks, learned about The Enneagram, bought the books, *The Fourth Way* and *In Search of The Miraculous* (I still have them), and went to the regular weekly meetings. This lasted only about four to six months because I was shocked at how misogynistic the group was and how much drinking went on. But, I did learn a practice called Self-Remembering, which came in handy much later in my life. At the time, I didn't get what this practice was supposed to achieve but I was struck by the effects it had on me.

During the time I was attending The Fourth Way School, I started practicing "Self-Remembering" throughout the day. It suited me to have a practice that I could intersperse throughout my day rather than finding a dedicated time each day. After a few months of doing this, I had an experience. It lasted two to three days. I was walking out the door when it was as if a light switch had been turned on in the whole world. Suddenly, everything grew brighter and I soon realized that I was outside of myself. I was behind my usual self, watching Tess in action. People began to tell me how special I was. An unknown woman ran across the road, through the traffic, to bow in front of me and ask me to pray for her. It wore off on the third day, and I had no idea what had happened. A few days later, when I went to the Gurdjieff group and told one of the leaders that this had happened, he laughed at me, and told me I was just making it up. He seemed to think I was looking for attention. I never went back.

About five years later I told a friend, whom I thought was an advanced spiritual man because he told me he had med-itated every morning for about an hour before he went to work. He also laughed at me, more kindly than the Gurdjieff man, but still he laughed indulgently at my story. So, I never mentioned it again. But, I didn't forget the extraordinary experience either. Many years later I read a book titled *Collision with the Infinite* by Suzanne Segal, and it described the experience precisely as I had experienced it. In her case the shift in perception lasted for years and caused her tremendous anxiety. In my case it faded in a few days and I remembered it as freedom beyond words. I was sorry it went away.

After the mockery, I became secretive about my experi-ences. Not that I had any for a long time afterwards, but even then I retained the fear of speaking about them to those who had not had such experiences and were likely to misunderstand. And besides, I felt the only reason to speak about such mat-ters was in order to get some understanding of what they were. One thing I learned is that it is not necessary to understand an experience for it to have its necessary effect. An experience, a spiritual experience, is a falling away of something, maybe a loss of a piece of ego and from then on one is changed by it, whether they understand what has happened or not.

This experience happened shortly before the marriage breakup and life became pretty untidy for a few years after that. I ended up living in the United States for eight years. Had you asked me during those years how my spiritual life was going, I would have told you that I had given up or forgotten all about. Anything I'd have called spiritual in those days looked like a luxurious add-on that I couldn't afford either energy wise or

2. NOTICING THE FOOTPRINTS

financially. I was taken up with keeping a roof over our heads and paying for transatlantic fares and phone calls.

Once again I had forgotten about the spiritual path and the radical questions of life, or so I thought at the time. Living in the United States offered me the opportunity to get some psychological counselling or therapy, something that was not available in Ireland at the time. I jumped at the opportunity. It was what looked relevant to me in terms of trying to get my mundane life on a functional footing. With hindsight, this was excellent preparation for the spiritual journey. For eight years I attended various therapies for varying periods of time. What I wanted was to find out what had gone wrong in my marriage. How had it come about that in less than ten years from the day I married the man whom I thought was to be my lifelong mate that we would end up in a state of non-communication despite having two children? I had no doubt but that both of us had entered the marriage in full sincerity, and we had been going around together for five years. I wanted to know what had been my part in this breakdown so that I would never again repeat it.

That was my goal, but not long into my very first round of therapy, it turned to questions about my family of origin. It took me a while to see that this was where the problem stemmed from because I was reluctant to dredge up what I thought of as old wounds that were no longer relevant. How wrong I was! I remember one evening during this phase when I was sitting in a group, and we each started sharing what our favorite Shakespeare quotation was. Mine, of course, was: To thine own self be true, and I once again remembered that I still did not know who or what I was beyond the conditioning of my childhood.

At this time, I read a book, *The Family,* by John Bradshaw, which was a real eye-opener for me. I discovered that my family was not unique, but a symptom of the society it existed in! And so was every other family! I identified myself as "the scapegoat" in our family and learned about the characteristics of "the scapegoat." Behaviors I had taken to be who I was turned out to be learned responses to my family environment and some behaviors had been foisted on me by those who needed a scapegoat for their own functioning. This gave me a bit of distance and detachment from family issues and some understanding of myself from a more objective point of view. It was very healing.

At one stage I participated in a yearlong therapy group with seven other women. This was the most beneficial therapy I experienced. We met for three hours every Thursday evening, led by a wonderful woman. The main thing I got from it was positive feedback. The rule was that we had to speak honestly to each other and only say what we meant sincerely. It is quite frightening at first to lay oneself open to honest feedback because we don't know what will be thrown at us. As a scapegoat, and coming from a Catholic culture where the attitude was to never pay a child, or indeed anyone, a compliment because it would give them "a big head," I had not received much positive feedback. I was acutely aware of all my faults and failings but not the positive attributes. This group spelled out to me attributes they found attractive about me as well as aspects of me that they thought unhelpful to me. Rather than see me as the failure who had left Ireland following a broken marriage, they saw me as a woman of strength and integrity. This had a profound effect on me. We were all trying to overcome our inherited or adopted dysfunctions and to get a realistic assessment of ourselves. It was amazing to find that we could help each other to heal ourselves, by simply being honest and sincere with each other. Nobody but ourselves can heal us, but it sure helps to find a group where everyone is working on their own healing. While I didn't think of this as self-inquiry or confrontation, practices I later learned are considered spiritual practices, this was a form of those practices.

During this time I became involved in a relationship with a man who had an alcohol problem. I didn't recognize the symptoms at first as I had not been exposed to this condition in my life, despite the fact that the stereotype of Ireland is as a nation of alcoholics. I started attending 12-step meetings. I learned a lot in this group also. My atheistic stance of my youth had softened when my children were born. Childbirth and babies just seemed too much of a mystery to me to be relegated to the notion of mere unthinking animals. I had become agnostic. However, I was able to go along with the notion of a Higher Power and found that adopting this attitude was extremely helpful and made life much easier. I did step four, "I made a searching and fearless moral inventory of myself," and I shocked some friends, mainly in Ireland, by writing or saying apologies for past events as step eight, "making amends," requires. They thought I had become some kind of religious fanatic. I learned a lesson from that too! Not everyone is on the same page as we are at the same time we are. I also learned that sometimes telling people what we are into, even after they have asked us, is taken as preaching or an attempt to convert them.

I turned forty while living in the US. This was a major turning point for me. I don't know why it should have been,

39

but I felt that my life would end before I was forty. Obviously, it didn't.

You know the saying: "life begins at forty"? Well, I had always thought that this was some kind of platitude to ease the burden of aging. But, it turned out to be true in my case and I have asked many women about it since and all, it seems, say that life after forty became easier for them, despite the fact that Gail Sheehy dubs it "the forlorn forties." Maybe it is the dying down of hormones or simply having arrived at a stage of accepting that the world can never satisfy our inner longing. Maybe we reach the stage of giving up on people-pleasing as our main modus operandi and start to live for ourselves —putting ourselves at the center of our own lives.

Around the time I turned forty I had a significant dream. I dreamt that I was walking alone in the woods and accidentally kicked some autumn leaves with my shoe only to reveal a golden key, the key to the kingdom of heaven. In the dream, I knew that this key had been deliberately placed there, knowing that I would be the only one walking in those woods at that exact time. This dream had a profound effect on me, in a positive way. I had no idea what it meant, but I knew it was good news. Ever since I was in my twenties I had been interested in dream interpretation and read many books on the topic. My understanding was there were two kinds of dreams: mundane and significant. A mundane dream is merely the mind processing daily life. Significant dreams have symbols that may not be immediately understandable but have a quality of being significant in some way. I had no doubt but that coming upon the key to the kingdom of heaven had significance for me. I had books on symbols, which I used to help me decode such symbols. I had also had a longtime interest in mythology and the work of Joseph Campbell which is one of the main ways I came to recognize the value and meaning of symbols. As Carl Jung said, dreams are a letter from our unconscious. Most people do not even read their mail.

I learned to read my dream mail to some degree, and it was a great help to me later on when I needed an understanding of what was going on with me. I knew I could trust the message of the dream world. All people dream. It is a universal phenomenon, an indication of our universal nature. I knew that there were universal symbols, such as mountains and rivers, and cultural symbols. A Buddhist might not receive a golden key to the kingdom of heaven as someone brought up in Christian culture would. We also have personal symbols. For instance, a black dog might mean friendship to one person and danger to another depending on their personal experience with dogs.

I read *An Unknown Woman* (A Journey to Self-discovery), by Alice Koller. I didn't just read it, I digested it. She finds herself at thirty-seven in a place not that different from me and not without some achievements. In her case, with a Ph.D. in Philosophy from Harvard, she had come to a point in her life where she says; "It has to stop. Can't I just stop, right now, and try to figure out what I'm doing? What should I be doing?" She went for three months to the island of Nantucket and lived alone in order to confront herself. "I must stop doing what I've been doing," she wrote. "And I can't stop doing it until I know what I do." She shares with her reader the intimate and painful details of her observations and her thought process in analyzing herself. And, as she says herself, because of her training in

41

philosophy she knew how to follow a thought down to its roots. It was an extraordinary idea to me at the time, to ask fundamental questions—*Why do I do what I do? What do I need other people for? How do I know when to trust my own feelings? Why do I conform so much even when it makes me unhappy? Why do I allow others to define who or what I am?* This was the beginnings of taking myself seriously and self-inquiry, even though at the time I had no idea where this might lead to, nor did I know then the term "self-inquiry."

It was around this time that I also read Sogyal Rinpoche's book, *The Tibetan Book of Living and Dying.* I agreed with him that we lived in a society (Western) which either denied death or lived in terror of it. But, that to not prepare for one's own death was foolish, like children putting their hands over their ears in order to not hear what the parents are saying. The idea was that the second half of life was to prepare oneself for death. We do not have to wait until it is upon us. Forty, I reckoned was about mid-way along the path of life and time to at least acknowledge consciously the inevitability of my own mortality.

When I think back on this period of my life what I remember most is what I used to call "waiting at the crossroads" periods. It seemed that I spent most of the time not knowing what to do next or where to turn. I simply read, waited, and got on with daily life. Yet, somehow, without me ever making a move, it seemed I would find myself checking out new directions, finding different authors, hearing different voices, going to spiritual events and for the most part rejecting what I found. I was developing a more refined idea of what possibilities life might hold, and what genuine spiritual development might look like during this time. I came across Joseph Campbell, the great mythologist, by seeing him being interviewed by Bill Moyers when I was visiting a friend. I found Henry David Thoreau, Thomas Merton, and Ralph Waldo Emerson.

I had lived in the United States for eight years, years of my children coming and going, and years of me healing myself with the benefit of therapies that were not available in Ireland at that time. I tried out all kinds of things, such as: writing to myself—a dialogue of self to self, getting a Master's degree in Critical and Creative Thinking, learning how to ask deeper questions, participating in a Dialogue group in the style of David Bohm, as well as the psychological counselling I wrote of earlier. Writing it out now, it looks like I was very busy at that time, but my overall memory of this period, and for several years after my return to Ireland was one of feeling like I was waiting, waiting for a direction to emerge. It seemed like nothing was happening except that time was passing; I was managing to keep daily life functional, and I was getting older, and death was out there on the horizon.

I had a full-time permanent pensionable job in the US. I had no intention of returning to Ireland, but some worrisome health issues arose and I had a dream. I awoke one morning from a snippet of a dream in which I was saying "When I lived in the US..." I knew then, without a shadow of a doubt, I was returning to Ireland. This happened in May, the end of the school year. Within a week, I put in my notice of resignation and returned to Ireland that summer. That was the summer of 1994.

That was the last dream I had for seven years. The loss of dreams was felt as a great loss by me. I didn't know that they would ever return, but in the loss of them I recognized how important they had been to my inner life. Without them my inner life had become two dimensional for the first time in my life.

Seeing our footprints going in the wrong direction, God can no longer abide his time. Like the Hound-of-Heaven He begins to chase us down. So what are our options now? Should we run faster, try to hide, or, as a true bull, daringly turn around and face Him, boldly ask Him what He wants of us? (Bernadette Roberts – Noticing the Footprints)

DISCOVERING THE PATH

3. Discovering the Path

I hear the song of the nightingale.
The sun is warm, the wind is mild,
willows are green along the shore – Here no bull can hide!
What artist can draw that massive head, those majestic horns?

In the third picture, the oxherd actually catches sight of the ox. Now, having started to practice, he glimpses the hidden powers to heal his suffering. But he does not yet understand the source of these powers and how to apply them in his search for peace and contentment. The verse, "I hear the song of the nightingale. The sun is warm, the wind is mild, the willows are green along the shore," suggests that the reality the oxherd glimpses is not something separate from the ordinary things that he experiences, even though he does not yet know this. (John Koller)

Back in Ireland—jobless, which at the time I thought was temporary but it turned out that I never again got a permanent or full-time or pensionable job—I got by with bits and pieces. The children were in college, pretty much grown up and independent. I turned forty-five that summer and the "waiting at the crossroads" continued for several years after my return to Ireland, only by now I had become desperate for something to happen and was sometimes met with periods of depression. I had fallen into a black hole. I looked like a failure to myself and assumed that others also thought so. Daily life wasn't offering me anything in the line of useful or financially rewarding work, the kids were grown up, and I didn't have many friends. Doing nothing was interpreted as negative by me and by the culture around me. Proudly we say, "We are doers." The successful, respected person is one who has something to show for their time. But, this "doing nothing" was not of my own choice; it had been imposed on me by circumstances beyond my control. That too, however, was a catch because the successful person is the one who seemingly has control over circumstances.

Suicidal thoughts began to arise, again. This was much worse than "waiting at the crossroads." This was…"my life isn't worth living any more, but I am trapped in not being free to bring it to an end because of the suffering it would cause to others." I felt isolated. I couldn't mention the suicidal thoughts to anyone because it would immediately have led to being brought to a doctor and probably would have landed me in a psychiatric unit, or I would have been met with a rational argument against doing it. I already knew all the arguments but feelings are different from thoughts and do not succumb to rationalization. What's more, because I have a cheerful personality, I did not come across as depressed.

My health condition was diagnosed and treatable. After a couple of years of the depression—which I didn't think of as depression, only that nothing was happening for me—I tried Prozac. It took about a week for it to kick in, then a few days of glorious happiness, and then I became "crazy." I mean crazy in the sense of feeling like I was all-powerful. Fortunately, due to some fairly painful feedback, I realized this and got myself off the Prozac immediately. That was the end of my flirtation with antidepressants. I wasn't reading much during this phase, at least, not as voraciously as I had in the past. My reading style changed. It became slower and I began to absorb what I was reading more deeply during this phase. I wasn't doing any other practices such as meditation or prayer during this period.

Thoreau's statement, "Most men lead lives of quiet desperation and go to the grave with the song still in them," fitted me perfectly at this point.

One book, however, which I had brought back from the States with me, did have an impact on me. I had come across the work of Douglas Harding while in the States but didn't get it. I knew he was writing about something important —*The Hierarchy of Heaven and Earth* —but I tried to understand it with my scientific mind. I did, however, get something from his writing, which I did not realize for many years. He said something like: *We do not own our own faces. Our face belongs to the world.* This made sense because he pointed out that when we are looking at another we see the face of the other, not our own. We never see our own face except as a reflection in a mirror. I also often pondered that when in a group I could see everyone's face except my own, and all the others could see my face, but not their own. But, I didn't have any idea as to what the significance to this observation might be and what he was trying to point out to his readers.

John Moriarty, an Irish mystic and another significant author in my journey, published his first book, *Dreamtime*, around the time of my arrival home. Like Douglas' work, I didn't get it but I couldn't stop reading it. I found that having read through the book something in me had changed. I couldn't say what but somehow it had a deep effect. He even said this some place in the book.

I often imagined visiting Douglas and John but felt that I couldn't until I got a better understanding of their work. I felt I should be able to discuss their writing with them if I visited them but was unable to articulate any questions or statements or even remember what I had read. I knew they were both writing about the thing that interested me most, but it was as if my brain had gone soggy and couldn't retain what I had read. With hindsight I know that both of them would have understood my problem of non-understanding but I didn't know that then. So, I never met either of them.

Towards the end of the depression, and of course it's only with hindsight that I can say this, I read a book of which I know neither the author's name or the title of the book, and it had a great effect on me. I think of it now as having heralded the end of the depression. It said that most people know what displeases them but rarely what brings joy, happiness, or peace to them. The author suggested that one keep a sharp eye on one's shifting emotions/feelings during the day to see what triggered joy. As soon as I left the house after reading the first few pages of it I came upon the first snow-drops of the year, announcing spring, and a wave of joy rose up in me. I felt that this had happened every year when I saw the first signs of spring, but I had not taken conscious note of it before. I started keeping a mental note of what brought this joy and noticed that it was something that rose and passed quickly. It didn't hang around all day, or even for more than a few minutes. I had never given it much credence before. So, moments of joy began to interrupt the depressive mood, or at least, I began to notice them. The contrast was startling. This was the beginning of discovering the footprints of the ox, or becoming consciously aware of how spirit communicates.

This feeling of joy was sometimes brought on by such events as: the laughter of a child, branches dancing in the wind, coming upon seasonal plants or a flower garden, the shape of clouds or the clouds racing each other across the sky, raindrops on the windshield of the car. This joy didn't necessarily repeat itself every time I came across these things. Its appearance was unpredictable and fleeting. I incorporated into my daily life the hunt for joy, or more precisely, the vigilance to notice when it visited. I also noticed the kinds of situations in which it never appeared.

While in the states I had come across a book by Thomas Merton: *Seeds of Contemplation*. This book opens with the following sentences, "Contemplation is the highest expression of man's intellectual and spiritual life. It is that life itself, fully awake, fully active, fully aware that it is alive. It is spiritual wonder. It is spontaneous awe at the sacredness of life, of being." I interpreted these experiences of joy as moments of contemplation. I already knew that contemplative moments happened spontaneously in the midst of everyday life and that it was something to be valued, but I had forgotten about it during the depression. I hadn't realized that one could be consciously on the lookout for them and that they could present as moments of unexpected joy.

I guess I could say that it was during this period that I became a contemplative in the world or became aware of my contemplative nature breaking through in daily life. It had always been present, but I had not recognized its value or what it pointed towards until this time.

I met a man, not long after my return to Ireland, whom I eventually married after we had spent many years developing a very good relationship with each other. His name was Seamus.

Having learned the lesson in my first marriage that leaving issues unresolved led to the death of real communication, this relationship was founded on honesty. It wasn't easy in the early years and there were many times where we almost came to an end. Fortunately for me, honesty was just as important to him. Indeed, it was simply native to him.

There were times during this depression, when I tried to believe in some notion of there being a life after death in some supposed heaven. But, I simply wasn't able to believe, or convince myself about it. I was trying to find some comfort for myself. I envied people who didn't suffer from the constant questioning that I lived with. Their lives seemed to be much simpler and happier than mine. But, the nature of my mind didn't allow me to believe something without which I had no evidence to back it up. I was eventually able to be honest with myself about this. At this time, while I mostly just got on with daily life, thoughts about and fear of death became frequent visitors. I felt like we were all dancing while The Titanic was sinking. I was desperately looking for a lifeboat—my own little lifeboat—while everyone around me was dancing to the music of life. This music had become an annoyance to me. I was gradually realizing that the world could no longer entertain me. I didn't want entertainment. I had a more pressing issue to deal with - death, my death. The world was a distraction from my big issue.

Now that I was fifty I began to take seriously the notion that the first half of life was for living in the world and the second half was for preparing for death. I became aware that the world could no longer satisfy me. I had "been there and done that," and I was tired of it. My mothering role was over; I didn't have a job that demanded attention or idealism, so I felt I was on the brow of the hill. I was also aware that no matter how good my relationship with Seamus was, there is very little any human being can do for another, in an ultimate sense. If he was feeling anxious about his job or feeling slighted by something that had been said to him, it was obvious that I couldn't do anything more than make him a dinner and welcome him home. I also realized that he could do nothing about my deep longing for something that I could not name. Once we acknowledge to ourselves that someone else cannot fix us, cannot alleviate our existential angst, it takes the pressure off the relationship and forces us to take full responsibility for ourselves. Maybe this is the definition of what it means to be a mature adult human being. Also, maybe it is the basic ingredient of a good relationship.

My father died the year I turned fifty. This was my first close involvement with death and maybe it was what triggered my greater seriousness about death, my own in particular. He was old. He was 96 and had lived a healthy life up to six months before his death. I saw how upset he was when he was first told that he had a terminal illness.

The subject of death had never been far from my mind in a way, ever since, when as a child of around eight or nine, a calf on our farm had died. Up to that point I had thought that everything that was born lived until it was old and had completed its natural lifespan. It was shocking to me that a calf died because it meant that a child could die, which meant that I could die at any time. Actually a friend of mine had died when I was around five. I even remember being at her funeral but somehow that didn't bother me at all. From the time of the death of the calf on, I was acutely aware that anyone could die at

any unexpected time, and there were plenty of stories throughout my life to remind me of this. But, I didn't know what or how
to think about it. It was simply a fact, and a very disturbing fact
at that. Sometimes I resented the fact that life was so precarious.
Sometimes I was angry at whatever had created the world and
me, that it had given us such an awful sentence to live with—the
death sentence. During this time it became increasingly difficult
for me to ignore it.

Sometimes I was simply stunned at the beauty of life
and the thought that it would all be taken away from us some
day. Sometimes I thought about ending it all and indulged in
fantasies about suicide as a way of alleviating the conflict. I
thought how simple it would be to just get it over with since I
would one day have to face my death anyway. And then I immediately thought about the suffering that would cause to my
family and after all I had long ago made a commitment to not
do that. Still, it kept coming back as an attractive idea.

This suicidal ideation was finally cured by a homeopathic remedy, I believe, because it stopped after taking a remedy
and has never again haunted me. This homeopathic consulta-
tion was also the only time I mentioned the suicidal ideation.
Towards the end of this period my reading began to point in a
different direction. I went looking for more "hard core" stuff. I
remember coming across the idea that suicide is an immature
act. It is a refusal to take on the big journey. Up to this time I
had not understood that there is the possibility of each of us
taking on "the big journey." I suspect that this is a problem for
many, who have not heard of the notion that there is some kind
of major journey available to us. In a secular society we don't
hear about these things or maybe don't recognize what is being

referred to when we do hear about it. We are likely to dismiss it as religious belief because it is so wrapped up and diluted in religious rituals and institutional dogma.

I started re-reading Buddhist, Sufi, and some Hindu literature in earnest. This kind of literature addressed the fact of us not having control over our circumstances and had things to say about that. A bigger picture was coming into view for me. I was absorbing what I read more deeply than I had in the past. I was applying the ideas to myself as opposed to collecting ideas.

One book that opened my mind to the nature of the spiritual path was *The Chasm of Fire*, by Irina Tweedie. I always sought out books by women in the hopes that I would better be able to read between the lines of what they were trying to communicate or be able to relate to their life histories. In the preface to her book Tweedie says: "When I went to India in 1961, I hoped to get instruction in Yoga, expected wonderful teachings: but what the Teacher mainly did was force me to face the darkness within myself, and it almost killed me. It was done simply--by using violent reproof, even aggression. My mind was kept in a state of confusion, unable to function properly. I was beaten down in every sense until I had come to terms with that in me which I had been rejecting all my life." There you have it! Not all that different from what Alice Koller said. "What could it be that we deny so vehemently that we are not even aware of it, and yet it is the very thing that causes our deepest and prolonged suffering?"

By now I knew death, my death, was my main conflict. I could see that this issue was the root cause of my suffering. The notion of death as annihilation confused me. I had heard the many references to eternal life and felt there must be something to them. Also, I just balked at the notion that we had been given this consciousness, this intelligence, this creative capacity, this capacity for love and joy, only to have it taken away from us. Either it must be a real nasty god who would do such a thing or I was overlooking or misunderstanding something fundamental, I reasoned.

I had come to accept that I couldn't just convince myself to forget about it or believe someone else' story or experience. It also became apparent that I couldn't just decide to face death directly. I could only think about it as an idea but the fear was palpable. I just couldn't accept annihilation as the full explanation despite the evidence that everyone dies. This impasse is what led to adopting various practices with a view to becoming able to face the darkness in me, that which I had been rejecting all my life, my own death. Now, here it was in my own family, my father's death. I didn't yet know that it was possible to "overcome" death while still in a body, "to die before you die" is an expression used in Zen literature.

In my reading I came across the notion that it was possible to prepare oneself for one's eventual death at any point in one's life. We didn't have to leave it until we were faced with it. This meant preparing for one's own death not merely by dwelling on it, and reading about death in general, but by deliberately taking down one's defenses against it.

Having started out thinking that the various spiritual traditions were separate lines of thought, I found that in fact they were all talking about the same thing. Death is a core issue in all religious/spiritual literature. It is the root cause of human suffering, the darkness we all have to face. The recommendation for an ethical lifestyle is to be found in all these traditions. All offer practices with a view to bringing about an inner change. All accept that there was a goal and that goal is the end of our personal suffering.

My reading led me to seeing the fundamental similarity of the various traditions rather than the differences. I started underlining key ideas in books and writing notes on the margins. With hindsight I can see that what happened was I started engaging more seriously with what I was reading as opposed to reading merely to gain information. The other thing was that the Internet became part of life. Amazon arrived and with it access to books that I could not otherwise have obtained. During this time I read Aldous Huxley's book, *The Perennial Wisdom* in which he points out the fundamental similarities of the various world spiritual traditions.

In 2003 my mother was found dead in bed. She had suffered a brain hemorrhage. Once again I was reminded of how unexpectedly death can arrive to anyone. It renewed my determination to be prepared for my own death regardless of how or when it came.

One day, about six months after my mother's death, I realized that my first boyfriend, Richard Rose, had not been at her funeral. This set me wondering if he had died, as at my father's funeral four years earlier he had told me about health issues he was having. Since he had always lived in my hometown, I was sure he would have heard about my mother's death and would have attended. I decided to Google his name. I am pretty sure it was the first time I Googled the name of anyone I knew. I was new to the internet.

I didn't find anything about him, but I did come across another Richard Rose—the one who founded The TAT Foundation in the USA. It was an evening in autumn when I came upon this site. Something happened within me while reading or trying to read it. I understood every word on the page but didn't understand what was being said. Each time I read a sentence something in me stopped, became unable to interpret intellectually, and in that gap a drip fell from inside my head into my chest/heart area. I repeated this reading of sentences often enough to see if this strange inner drip would continue and it did. I became alarmed and wondered if there was something wrong with me physically. I wondered if there was some disease in which the brain dissolved and dripped away. The drips fell into the chest area as if it were a basin into which a tap was dripping. It was not unpleasant, only startling.

I went to bed wondering about this unusual phenomenon and I had no doubt that it was something on the site or the words that had triggered this experience in me. I knew that there was something important for me in this site, plus the fact that I had come upon it "accidentally." The following morning I went back to that site to try to figure out what it was about. And that is the beginning of the next chapter in this story.

Since he is now too close to escape there is no choice but to turn, look Him in the face, and bluntly put our question to Him. What we never planned on, however, was the nature of this face-to-

Face encounter. Just seeing God face-to-Face is all it takes to turn anyone's life around – forever! For a moment we even lose sight of ourselves. God, however, never loses sight of us. He alone knows what He has created, knows His plan for our eternal destiny knows the "Way" and can bring us there. But what, we ask, could God possibly get out of this? Now no man can fathom God's love for all He has created, yet all He asks is that we love Him back. This is all He wants, all He has ever asked of us. And what is our reply? (Bernadette Roberts – Catching Sight of the Ox)

STARTING THE JOURNEY

4. Catching hold of The Ox

I seize him with a terrific struggle.
His great will and power are inexhaustible.
He charges to the high plateau far above the cloud-mists,
Or in an impenetrable ravine he stands.

The fourth picture shows that the oxherd has now caught hold of the ox, using the bridle of discipline to control it. This symbolizes the rigorous discipline required of the Zen practitioner. Although he now realizes that the power to transform his life lies within him, in his Buddha-nature, all of his previous conditionings are pulling and pushing him in different directions. Holding the rope tightly means that he must work hard to overcome his bad habits of the past that developed through the ignorance, hatred, and craving that gave rise to all of his afflictions. (John Koller)

Below are the words I had come across when I discovered TAT. The homepage of this site hasn't changed since that fateful night for me:

"The highest form of spiritual work is the realization of the essence of man…" "You never learn the answer; you can only become the answer."

"My purpose is to outline a system which will prove itself as it goes along, and which will reward us at any point along the line by finding for us a more disciplined and skillful mind, and a mind that is more aware of itself."

—Richard Rose

The life of the spiritual seeker is often a solitary affair. However, there are friends to find, books to read, and information to share. The TAT Foundation and its spiritual search site offer a place for genuine philosophical and spiritual inquiry on all levels, modelled on the principle that cooperation and interaction with fellow inquirers can expedite a seeker's own investigation. Within these pages, you will find an introduction to Richard Rose and his system for spiritual achievement, the continuing work of the TAT Foundation, and esoteric books and recordings of value to those interested in the search for Reality. The depth of friendship and a unique set of principles without the dogma—these form the basic precepts of TAT® videos, audio, publications, and events.

There is something shockingly direct about these words. For all the books I had read up to this point I had not heard clearly that: "The highest form of spiritual work is the realization of the essence of man...."

What did I think I had been doing during all my decades of reading and trying out various practices? The essence of man—what am I essentially? It must be something to do with what the various teachings are referring to in words and phrases such as "eternal life" or "immortality" or the "mystery of life," I reasoned. And what can he mean by "You never learn the answer; you can only become the answer."? I realized then that I had been trying to find the answer or understand it. But, "become the answer?" What can that mean? It suggests that there is an answer but it is an answer that cannot be learned or understood, I reasoned, an answer that is found only through inner transformation.

Such thoughts and questions led me to dig deeper into this site and over time into the various links to it. I had caught hold of the ox. I spent the next two years reading TAT related material. They had been producing a monthly magazine—The Forum—since the early 1970's. The archives are available online. I read most of them. There was a book titled *After the Absolute*, which was about the life of Richard Rose and his group of students. I read that. I ordered many of the books published by them, mainly written by Richard Rose, and I studied them deeply. This included a little booklet titled *Meditation*, which altered completely my idea of what meditation was really about. In it he talked about "going within." I got it that "within" was where the "essence" was located. But, it wasn't that easy to do the "going within," and besides I was never confident that my various efforts were right. I didn't know if I was doing it right. I now know there is no "right," but then I thought there must be some particular method that I wasn't getting the hang of. I now know that "going within" is the uniquely personal way that each one starts to locate their inner thoughts and feelings, to allow them to come into view.

Nowadays I am often asked "how exactly do you go within?" People want an exact methodology, but the problem is that it is something unique to the individual. You have to find your own way of looking and seeing what is coming up within yourself. Usually, what we overlook is something that is so familiar that we have become immune to its presence. The "familiar" is our intimate thought streams, emotional patterns, and assumptions. But although the journey within is unique to each of us, the practice of self-inquiry gives us hints about how to do this for ourselves.

The last page of Rose's booklet gives summary notes under two headings: Levels of Meditation and Preparation for Meditation. This one page gave me more information and guidance than all the books I had read over decades, but I also think that if it hadn't been for all the other reading I might not have benefitted so much from this succinct summary. Clarity about the goal, what spiritual seeking was about, and how to facilitate this end was taking place in me. Richard Rose's description of meditation is "productive thinking," in other words what we nowadays call self-inquiry.

By the time I came across this website, I had already given up on finding any lasting or meaningful satisfaction in the world. I had a good relationship with my partner (husband later), but I knew that it didn't even touch my deepest anxieties and confusions. I understood at an even deeper level now that he couldn't save me from death or anxiety or insecurity or meaninglessness. I also knew that all the wealth in the world couldn't make me happy. I didn't have any responsibilities in the world in the sense that my children were grown up and had left for their own lives. I hadn't found a "cause" to devote my time and energy to. I had nothing to complain about, but it was just so unpromising. I had already made a commitment that I would not commit suicide, and the ideation had ceased, so I decided I simply had to live my life out as best I could without expectation of any real satisfaction or joy.

Yet...how is it that I knew the taste of joy? How could it be that I knew this so well and yet couldn't access it? I had had a dream not long before this fateful night when I was upset to awaken because the love in the dream was so real, and of such an order and quality as was not available to me in daily life. It seemed that the gap between what was available in daily life and what I knew inwardly was a yawning canyon, a heartbreaking teaser.

I felt guilty about the fact that I was so dissatisfied because on the surface I had it all: a healthy body, a caring family, well-adjusted children, a partner I liked and who was good to me, and so on. It seemed the more I became aware of how much I had been given in life the greater the underlying dissatisfaction came to the fore. Gratitude and inner emptiness seemed to go, paradoxically, hand in hand. Not until I read something attributed to The Buddha did I clearly identify my condition. His question was "How come I, who has it all, still suffer?" He was from a privileged background, and as a young man became aware of the human condition as being one of suffering.

It was like getting a diagnosis for my condition. I wouldn't have named my condition as suffering as I had other ideas of what this word meant. The Buddha's definition of suffering I realized referred to what in the West we call "existential angst." I had not distinguished the difference between suffering and pain. My reading now went along the lines of trying to understand what "suffering," or existential angst really is and what is at the root of it. I read that there are two kinds of suffering: suffering that is inherent in being a human in the world, which is what I took was meant by pain, and the suffering caused by ego. The ego suffering is caused by misidentification of what we are, the belief that what we are is a world created creature (conditioning) and we can do something about it. This is the root cause of our existential angst. There is only one cure for it, correction of the misidentification, which amounts to loss of wrong concepts and false beliefs. The loss of falsity leads to Truth. This is experienced as an inner transformation which culminates in what is known variously as: Self-realization or Enlightenment or Christ Consciousness, Moksha.

I was now developing a clearer idea of what spiritual work is about and what the goal of it is. Now I began to look seriously at how I could do this work on myself. The word ego began to loom large in my mind, trying to get a handle on what it really was and to see it in action in myself. I knew I was looking for what was "not ego" but had to be able to see ego before I could get to what was not ego. Eckhart Tolle has a good chapter on ego in his book *A New Earth*, so there is no need for me to go into it here. His description of ego in action helped me identify ego in myself. It gave me a picture of how it manifested. Since I knew that everyone acted out of ego, I learned a lot about my own ego from observing others. It's a strange idea when you first come across it, to see that everyone is acting from a false identity, and not aware of it. It's a whole new view of human interactions.

Having acquired a clearer idea of ego I sought out books written by women in the hopes that I would get a better idea of how it manifested in women, if indeed there was a difference. I came across Pema Chodron and Ani Tenzin Palmo, both of the Tibetan Buddhist tradition. I found them very helpful. I read *Reflection on a Mountain Lake*, by Ani Tenzin Palmo, and a few books by Pema Chodron. Both women were born and grew up

in the West and adopted Tibetan Buddhism as their wisdom
path and became nuns. Pema was married and raised two
children before entering the monastery. A few of her books that
I read include: *The Places that Scare You, Start Where You Are,
The Wisdom of No Escape,* and *Taking the Leap.* She has written
many other books as well.

I did find something more accessible in reading the
books written by women, although I have to admit that what
they were saying was no different from what the male authors
I had been reading were saying. Maybe it was the way it was
said or that they used examples from daily life in a way that
I could relate to. Or, maybe it was simply that I was ready to
hear these teachings in a deeper way than I had been up to this
point. Incidentally, in Ani Tenzin Palmo's book, *Reflections on a
Mountain Lake,* she has a chapter on Women on the Path which
is valuable reading for any woman on the path. She explains,
from the Buddhist perspective, how it came about that women
have had such little influence in the traditional settings where
these teachings are passed on. What she says applies equally to
the Christian tradition and I suspect all the other traditions.

Hunting the ego and looking for what was not ego now
became the game, and somewhere in the mix was Jesus' statement that I had learned as a child: "Blessed are the meek, for
they shall inherit the earth." Meek – humble, the opposite of
ego? So, ego must be related to pride?—I wondered.

I had spent most of my life trying to be a person of
integrity, and I knew that meant not being prideful, but I just
couldn't see where I was missing the mark. I thought I had
dealt with pride. I had replaced it with gratitude, but still it was

obvious to me that this ego was not just operating in order to function but controlling my life, most of the time. I began to see that ego and pride were the same thing. This came as quite a shock as I had thought I had dealt with pride in myself. I had for a long time been practicing an attitude of gratitude for the various successes in my life as an antidote to pride. Now, with this new found self-observation I wondered if there was anything other than ego or pride operating in me. At some point I came to realize that there are two kinds or levels of pride, pride in relation to the world and pride in relation to who we are, or you might say God, or our source. Not realizing or admitting that EVERYTHING is given to us, our bodies, our very lives are not of our own making but given by THE GIVER of all things, is pride in relation to our source. Pride in relation to the world is taking credit for our various successes. This worldly pride is really us thinking that we are in control of our lives. For me recognizing the difference between these two levels of pride or ego was a milestone in returning to my True Nature, although they are but two aspects of the one thing.

According to Buddhist literature the roots of the ego are greed, anger, and ignorance, meaning ignorance of our true nature. These are the chains that bind us. Sometimes the words used, such as, greed, throw us off what we are looking for. For example, I didn't see myself as greedy or angry but looking more closely at the idea of greed I could see that it meant wanting what I wanted. I wondered how I could stop wanting things to be a certain way. I want my children to be well. I want to be well myself. But, is this greed? It seemed impossible to stop wanting such things and yet the teachings were saying that this is what I must do. Over time it became clear to me how I was using every situation to get what I wanted, and that this is what everyone else does also. I didn't realize that this was what I was doing because we have learned to cover this up with socialization and manners and niceties. This might look like a very strong statement but on careful examination it turned out to be the case. We are socialized to cover up our inner motives, to such an extent that we have lost sight of them ourselves. Everyone is playing the same game, getting what we want while playing nice.

Self-inquiry takes us below the level of socialization; it takes us to the depths of our own motivations and assumptions. It takes us below the level of what is glossed over in normal socialization. And, anger…anger isn't just being in a rage; it has more subtle manifestations such as irritation, annoyance, and resistance to what is. The root of all anger is in resistance to "what is" in favor of what we want. Just because we don't express it doesn't mean that it isn't there, within us. Anger and greed are listed among the seven deadly sins as taught in the Christian tradition, so I had thought about these already but I had understood them as non-expression of these behaviors. As a woman I had been socialized to not express anger. "Nice girls aren't angry." Now I started to look at them from the perspective of being experienced internally, regardless of whether they are expressed or not. It became clear to me that not expressing my irritation or anger didn't mean that it didn't exist in me. All that I had been doing was suppressing the expression of these emotions. I also came to see that not only had I learned to suppress the negative emotions, but also the positive. Seeing this let me understand what is meant by "the inner child" in some of the recent therapeutic literature. There is an aspect of us, a childlike, spontaneous, playful aspect that has been suppressed in favor of being responsible and logical. This too had to be recovered.

Enquiry

Self-inquiry is the business of uncovering all that has been suppressed, not necessarily to share with others but in order to be ourselves, right down to the roots of our being. It was with this kind of exploration that I set about taking note of everything that I resisted or suppressed, (including having fun for no other reason than having fun) everything I did not want, and everything I did want… but at a more subtle level and in more precise detail than anything I had done before. I understood that my job was not necessarily to change these things (habits), but to notice them because until I noticed them, I could not see what was at the root of them, could not see the ways in which I was hobbling myself. With hindsight I'd say that this was "going within" to use Richard Rose's term, but at the time it didn't look like anything significant to me.

I had also come across ideas about thought processes and the genesis of thought in Richard Rose's teachings. There were ideas about observer and witness that kept coming up. I was trying to locate something in myself that could relate to such ideas. I wondered if the observer was "not-ego." My efforts at observing, especially observing the thought streams were proving that this was not easy. Immediately I noticed a thought stream, another thought stream arose commenting that I was now observing the first thought stream and of course the first thought stream disappeared. This would be followed by another stream of thoughts about how ineffective I was at this or how impossible this practice was. Round and round went the thought streams, at high speed, with barely a gap between them.

70

I figured I did not understand what was meant by being The Observer. I tried watching myself washing the dishes, making an effort to concentrate my attention on the dishwashing but thoughts about observing myself washing the dishes took over. It seemed impossible to me to simply observe activities around me without inner commenting taking over, and associative thought streams arising.

This is not an easy phase, but it is a necessary one because at the beginning you really see "monkey mind" in action, the untamed ox within. But, with perseverance, in your own way, that ox will be tamed. This is the message of all the great teachings. Richard Rose used the expression "leave no stone unturned" and spoke about the effort needed on the spiritual path. For me, this was the stage which was most effortful for me. I found this self-observation and constant questioning of every aspect of myself hard work. I didn't feel like I was making any progress, not that I knew what progress looked like. But, once this self-observation started I couldn't go back to being unconscious of what was going on within me. As I said earlier, I had already given up on finding any satisfaction in the world so this was the only hope of finding anything meaningful to do with my life left to me. So, I had put my faith in the process, or these teachings, you could say. It wasn't that I thought of what I was doing as having faith or trust in these teachings but with hindsight I can say that that is what was happening during this phase. The various spiritual teachings actually say that it's important to have enough faith or trust in them to do the work or to follow the recommended practices. This was my experience also.

Looking back now I can see how different this phase was from the years leading up to it in which I had given up on ever finding satisfaction in this life. This was a phase of commitment, not in the sense that I made a conscious commitment but that all other options had closed for me, and all I was left with was this one last final option. It wasn't an option really. It was the only thing left.

My attention had been grabbed by a new possibility. Mind you, the possibility which seemed to lie in the direction of being able to observe the mind and uncover what had been suppressed looked rather daunting. But, it was the only possibility left as everything else had fallen away from me. While this questioning that was taking place in me, along with my efforts to adopt recommended practices, "seeing" (Douglas Harding's practice), solitary retreats, etc., I began to experience nightmares. I didn't know that I knew what a nightmare was until I started to experience them. I had no memory of having nightmares as a child. I had had my share of bad dreams during my life, but these were of a different order. I do not now remember the content of them but at the time I articulated them to myself as visitations from the demons of the depths. They were not frequent, maybe once or twice per year, and they were interspersed with another kind of dream which was the opposite. They were dreams of such beauty and love and joy that it saddened me to have to wake up in the morning and come back from them.

I think the main reason I remember these nightmares is that Seamus (my husband) was very upset by how disturbed I would be when I woke from them. Because, as I have mentioned, I had always paid attention to dreams and especially to the symbols in dreams, I knew that something was happening in the depth of the psyche. I was both comforted and frightened by this but still did not associate it with the practices and reading I was doing. I still did not realize that I was on a path or journey at this point. All I was doing was following my nose and my nose had led me to self-inquiry as the only option left to find some kind of happiness or meaning in my life.

At Easter 2005 I went on a Goenka Vipassana, 10 day silent retreat. It was the first time I had experienced ten days without talking. I really liked it. I had some very intense dreams which I have forgotten. On one of the last days, as the morning bell rang to call us to meditation, I became the vibrations caused by the ringing of the bell. It was startling but not upsetting—just odd. I remained like that for hours. What I mean is that I was not there, only some kind of receptive center for all vibrations, sounds and sights. Then it wore off and I thought little more about it. I remember it because I had made a few notes during the retreat and it was among them.

The technique being taught was one of observing the sensations in the body. After ten days of this I remained permanently aware of the flow of sensations in the body. I became aware of the constant arising and passing of sensations in the body. With self-observation I became able to discriminate between different classes of sensations and learned to notice them without anxiety or judgement. It was easy to discriminate between sensations caused by interaction between the body and its environment such as heat and cold, hunger, pain due to some physical discomfort and sensations caused by emotions, which usually emerged in the solar plexus or the neck and face. It was also easy to notice that sensations varied in intensity and duration. In my notes I have underlined a

73

statement made during the retreat: Equanimity is gained by objective observance of sensations and not reacting to them. I longed for equanimity and maybe this is why I became adept at sensation watching so quickly.

The last words S. N. Goenka said at the end of the video talk given every evening at the retreat was "No me, No mine, No I." I didn't know what he was talking about but somehow the phrase sunk into my mind like a mantra or maybe a koan.

I decided early in the summer of 2005 that I would go to the US to a TAT weekend retreat, mainly to see for myself if they were a group of people with "high integrity," as I sensed from their website and my reading of the materials they produced or recommended. I had not yet made contact with anyone in the group. It was also early in my internet days and one heard a lot about abuses and dishonesty that could be hidden on the internet. This was also a time when a lot was coming out in the media about the abuses in the various religions and spiritual groups. I needed to check out TAT for myself. An old friend, who lived in the US, accepted my need to check out this group and took seriously my concerns decided to come with me for the weekend. Even with a friend, I was nervous going. To be finally meeting with the group who had come to mean so much to me held the possibility that I might have been wrong in my assessment of them. I was also nervous because I felt that I did not intellectually understand the teachings. What if they asked me to explain something or assumed that I understood what they were saying?

Looking back over my notes from the summer of 2005 they are filled with dreams along the theme of finding myself in a conflicting situation. One dream was that I was ordered by the president of The United States, under the guise of an invitation that I couldn't refuse, to attend a party in The White House. The party was a Capital Punishment party and I was expected, compelled, to participate in the activities. In another dream I was compelled to marry a man who would cost me the friendship of my children and family and friends. And, I didn't even count those ones as nightmares! The underlying theme of these dreams was about me being authentic to my own values, regardless of what it cost. Integrity, my integrity, was being challenged. Was I willing to stand up for what really mattered to me?

Shortly before my trip to The US, a couple of friends visited. One of them asked, while the other was in the bathroom, why I was going on the trip. I told her about the upcoming retreat and about how I had come across the group. She had known my original Richard Rose. When the other friend returned from the bathroom she said, rolling her eyes in disbelief, "She's going to the US to a group with the name of an old boyfriend." I could see they were both horrified. I learned once again to be cautious about what I said and to whom, about this path. But I was made uneasy by their reaction, uneasy to the point of wondering about cancelling the whole trip. Maybe it was crazy or a wild-goose chase. The night before the trip I took out my Tarot cards. I had Tarot cards for about thirty years and consulted them very occasionally when in doubt about what to do in a particular situation. The card I picked that night said something like: The trip will be successful, necessary even, and will bear fruition but not immediately. There is much work to be done.

Having seen God, we are so overjoyed at being caught we rue all the time we wasted without God on our tail. Quickly we become friends with much exchange of affection and delightful treats. The only blip in this scenario is when God suddenly goes off, disappears on us and we grow anxious, miss Him terribly. Now we must forage for ourselves and spend lonely nights. In time, however, we learn to patiently wait out these absences; our trust is becoming unshakable and too, we are learning to see Him on ever deeper levels – even, see Him in the dark! And, with every sudden return His light and love become ever more exalted – totally worth the wait! But who can understand the demands of exchange in such a great love as this? Love, after all, demands equality – no happiness in an unequal exchange. To be given everything and return nothing is the anathema of love -better not to love at all. Yet all we can give God is what is ours, what we ourselves have made, which is nothing compared to everything God has given us. All we have to give God is what He has made – ourselves, our whole being. He can take it, exchange it, recreate or transform it, even to the point of no return. It is this supernatural refashioning that becomes the make-or-break of the journey; this is the ordeal of becoming God-proven, if it can be put that way. This is the ordeal-of-ordeals. (Bernadette Roberts – Getting Hold of the Ox)

THE INNER STRUGGLE

5. Taming the Ox

The whip and rope are necessary,
Else he might stray off down some dusty road.
Being well-trained, he becomes naturally gentle.
Then, unfettered, he obeys his master.

The fifth picture shows that disciplined practice can overcome the bad habits of previous conditioning and bring one into accord with the true nature of reality. Although discipline is still needed because the old habits of mind still have power, living in greater awareness of the true reality gives one the energy and direction to live a wholesome life. Now the ox willingly follows the oxherd home, meaning that the separation between oneself and true reality is being overcome. (John Koller)

I did go to the TAT September weekend intensive retreat in 2005. The theme of the weekend was: Crossing the Mind-Bridge. The blurb on the site advertising it went as follows:

> Is the individual destined to live in darkness regarding his existence, purpose, and meaning? Is the only alternative to trust someone who claims to know, or believe some wise words from the twilight of history? Or is it possible for the individual to use his mind, the realm of doubt and uncertainty, to transcend the darkness and discover the truth? Beyond the mind is a golden find, as Richard Rose and others throughout history have testified. It can be discovered by those who seek with persistent determination. The TAT 2005 Fall Workshop is an opportunity to meet a wonder-

ful group of fellow-seekers, including a few individuals who have found answers. Not hiding
behind robes or rituals, nor selling their message
for money, they are available for this weekend to
help you in your quest to discover answers for
yourself.

How could I resist such a blurb? It was exactly what I was looking for, and by the time I left that retreat I knew I had made a
find beyond my highest hopes. What I got was precisely what
it said in the blurb. I had found a group with integrity, according to my idea of what that was. This had always been what I
could recognize and wanted, but didn't know how to develop or
complete in myself. I knew there was still work to be done on
myself. I now understood, for the first time, that I was what is
known as a spiritual seeker, and much to my surprise I learned
that the world is full of such ones. I learned that enlightenment
isn't just for exotic persons from by-gone eras. This potential is
in everyone and this is what all seekers are seeking. I came to
understand "enlightenment" as the fulfilment of our potential
for growth in integrity. There were a number of people present
who claimed to have reached the end of seeking because their
deepest, most radical questions had been answered. While I
didn't actually understand what this meant, I was impressed by
their integrity.

During this weekend someone said to me "You're as
good a candidate for final realization as I have ever met." I was
appalled! Despite all my reading and seeking I was still thinking
in terms of becoming a person of integrity. I was still thinking
that the job of improving the person continued until the day

we died. It was hard to take in the idea that this could come to an end before death and that this could happen to me. My assumptions of what the goal of spiritual seeking was, was really challenged. I also harbored the notion of The Final Realization as being something that happened only very rarely. During this weekend I began to accept or at least entertain the notion that Self-realization, (awakening, enlightenment, Christ consciousness, whatever word is used to refer to the same thing), the recognition of and identification of our True Nature, is possible for EVERYONE. It was shocking to me to think that I might be of the same ilk as Jesus or The Buddha.

This statement was a game changer for me because it brought up many assumptions and challenges to my thinking at the time. I have noticed that I was never aware of my assumptions until something challenged them. I had never heard anyone speak directly and openly about Self-realization before. This was a big challenge to my understanding of what spiritual development was about. Despite my rejection of Catholic teaching I still had the assumption that spiritual life was about leading a good life, developing integrity, so that I would be rewarded when I died, or maybe get to a higher level of evolution next time around if I accepted the notion of reincarnation.

This incident is also an example of how we may understand something at one level or in one context but not in a different context. My belief that Jesus, the Buddha, and the saints were of a different essence than me, assumed that there were different classes of humans. I was not aware that I thought that. Because at the same time I believed that we are all "children of God" or fundamentally the same. I was beginning to notice my inner contradictions.

81

A deeper or more comprehensive understanding of ideas, spiritual teachings in particular, happens as we begin to notice our own inner contradictions. The collapse of contradictions leads to integration.

This incident led me to take a look at the teachings of Jesus from a different perspective—to see them as guidance and practices for spiritual fruition, not as guidance for living in the world, which had been my understanding up to this point. A new level of discernment was arising in me, but it is only with hindsight that I can say this. And if I was to take seriously his teaching that we are all "children of God," does this not mean that I have a natural inheritance to my source, the same inheritance that he had and that everyone has? I had been shown the need for "the whip and the rope." It became obvious to me for the first time that I was full of inner contradiction. Shocking eye-opener!

Following the weekend intensive, I stayed on at what they referred to as The Farm, in a cabin, which had been built for the express purpose of spending time alone. It's what is known as an isolation retreat, a practice recommended by Richard Rose. Two days is all I did. It was the first time I spent time alone for the express purpose of looking within myself. My friend who had travelled with me also spent a couple of days in another cabin on the other side of the farm.

The idea behind spending time alone is to stop or reduce external stimuli in order to allow what is hidden in the psyche to come into attention. TAT recommended what they considered solitary retreats as a practice. This simply meant creating time alone in one's life. It could be for a few hours, or days or weeks. The conditions didn't matter so long as it was a safe quiet place.

Spending time alone was not new to me, but spending it looking at my thoughts and observing my emotions was new. My understanding was that self-observation was necessary in order to uncover the hidden contradictions that I was now becoming aware of. It was not long after this retreat that I began to see the close connection between thoughts and emotions. I had thought that emotions generated thoughts but found that it was really the other way around.

With hindsight I can say that spending time alone, observing my inner world, was one of the most profound and beneficial practices I took on. After returning home I did two-night solitary retreats about once every six weeks. I fitted it into my life with little or no disruption to my own schedule or anyone else's. This weekend, in the cabin at The Farm, had a profound effect on me; taming the ox had begun, but I was not aware of this at the time. It's only in looking back over my journey that I can see this.

The first time I spent two days alone observing my thoughts and feelings, something unexpected and shocking did come up. Decades earlier a strange incident had happened in my life. I, for no reason it seemed, became strangely exhausted while visiting friends with my boyfriend at the time. There was a crowd of young people in the house and a lot of activity going on. I went to bed. While in bed, I had what I thought was a very vivid half- asleep, half-awake dream, in which my boyfriend came into the room and had sex with me. After I got up, my boyfriend said this had not happened, so we wrote it off as a dream. Now, after all those years thoughts about this day kept coming up and I interpreted that what had happened was that I had been drugged and raped, right in the middle of family and friends. I don't know for sure if this did actually happen, but during my first solitary retreat this looked like the only explanation. This was a shocking realization or interpretation for me. I was deeply disturbed by it.

Afterwards I told a few friends about my "shocking realization." They were very sympathetic and caring, to the point that I realized that this could become a big issue if I allowed it to develop that way. I would be seen as the victim who had been drugged and raped. I reasoned that since this had happened decades earlier, and as I hadn't realized what happened I wasn't traumatized by it.

This "memory" did however alert me to the question of what else might I not know about myself. What else might come up given the opportunity? I made a decision that I had to face whatever might come up if I wanted to get to the truth of my being. This was not an easy decision, considering what I had recently "realized" about myself. In fact, I remember arriving at this decision with a feeling of anger and determination. God only knew what other events might come to light, I thought, but I was going to get to the root of my suffering no matter what it cost. I felt I couldn't live with myself as I was any longer. The need for whip and rope, to tame the ox of my personal ignorance about myself, had arrived. I felt angry at my own unconsciousness and naivety. The lasting effect of this "memory" was the determination that arose in me.

A few years later I came across this passage in a book titled Music and Madness, by Ivor Browne: "It is now clear from much recent research that when a formed memory of this kind is retrieved, it is reassembled from a number of inputs all over the brain, from various times past, and therefore is essentially a new creation. It is therefore quite unreliable as a factual record of the past."

I have since come to wonder if this was indeed a false memory, because afterwards a couple of other memory tricks happened to me, all of which had the effect of causing a change in me. In this first case the change was to make me committed to doing this work on myself.

There were other times, later on in this journey, when I felt my mind was playing tricks on me and I wondered about my sanity. It was as if the ground beneath me was turning to quick sand. An example of this was a time when for a couple of days I found myself remembering two incidents in my life, about five years apart which had occurred decades earlier and which I had not connected. The two memories kept repeating for a couple of days. Then I decided to look at them and realized that both were incidents in which I had acted courageously and with authenticity in situations where I expected to be rejected for it but instead had gained respect for and inner strength from my actions. I had had the courage to go against my usual people pleasing conditioning. On seeing this connection, I found I became more courageous and authentic in my behavior with others. I simply became more authentic without having to work at it. A change had been effected in me.

"To thine own self be true..." had always been my inner slogan, only now it had taken hold of me. Courage and determination had arisen. I could no longer live with myself as I was. I had become acutely aware of my suffering and could see that my whole life had been laced with suffering. I simply had to bring this suffering to an end. To whatever extent I had succeeded in keeping this suffering at bay in the past, I could no longer deny it. The suffering had become sharp. It was as if now, all I had read about digging deep or going within or facing our shadow made sense for the first time.

The shadow side of us has to be faced, said Carl Jung. That which we are unaware of and suppress and abhor in ourselves has to be faced. All spiritual teachings speak about the difficulty of the path and until this time I had not understood what this meant. To face our own demons, ignorance, abuses, selfishness, unconsciousness (that within us which we most hate) is the most difficult part of the path, because we have to own it. The reality of coming to see and face my inner contradictions, incompatible beliefs, petty selfishness, half-baked ideas and naivety was awful. I could hardly believe that I had lived my whole life in such ignorance. To say that this stage was humbling is an understatement. It was devastating. I was seeing that my whole life had been a lie, based on false beliefs and assumptions and unconsciousness. Self-inquiry was the only tool I had to bring this lie to an end. Grace had given me the courage and determination to work at it. I felt as if I was melting. The hard shell that had been me was cracking.

For all the therapy I had done when I had been digging into my past and my life and I thought I was digging deep, this was of a different order. What self-inquiry was uncovering was a deeper layer and the effects were felt as seismic.

Oddly, the more I was falling apart inside, the more grounded and stable I was becoming in my personality. It was strange.

One of Richard Rose's sayings was that we have to back away from untruth. We cannot approach the truth directly as we might any other goal in life. I understood this to mean that since the mind is the container of the untruths, self-inquiry is the tool with which to find them and not until they are found or seen can they be "backed away from." What I didn't know at the start of this phase was that when two contradictory beliefs or assumptions came to the surface, either one of them didn't stand up to reason or they were both subsumed into a broader interpretation. This was the start of a process. I came to see that anything that has been suppressed or gone unrecognized still has a hold on one in an unconscious way and allowing it to become conscious takes the power out of it.

There is the danger at this stage of getting lost in psycho-analyzing and trying to fix past events or redress the wrong that had been done, because what is suppressed is often what we perceive as the wrongs that have been done to us. Ideas of right and wrong, should and shouldn't, are prime fodder for ego. The problem I found here was that I had to come to accept the past as it was and not get distracted by any ideas of right or wrong, what should or shouldn't have happened. I mention this because I see how easy it is for us to confuse psychological healing with self-inquiry.

During the TAT retreat I had heard an expression used by Richard Rose: "afflictions to the ego," which I interpreted to mean, anything that upset me. I also heard that becoming aware of afflictions to the ego was a way of seeing it in action. So, I could use any upset as an opportunity to look for the underlying cause of the upset. The things to look for were the assumptions, beliefs, expectations, motivations, and so on. Reacting to what goes on at the surface level prevents or distracts us from delving into the root cause of the reaction. Making the shift to seeking out the root causes of our reactions as opposed to reacting or fixing our emotional reactions is the beginning of genuine self-inquiry. One has learned to look within, and with this shift I found that there arose a new level of consciousness in me. What I found in myself wasn't always pleasant and it was often surprising. Coming to see the competing desires, the conflicting assumptions, the half-baked beliefs and unnecessary fears that normally dictate our experience of life is a real eye-opener.

I had the belief that paying "too much attention" to my actions and reactions was self-centered and therefore ego enhancing. The idea was that one of the signs of a big ego was someone who thought about themselves a lot. My husband used to tell me to leave well enough alone. I also worried that this might be dangerous, playing with my sanity.

However, I became able to see that paying attention to one's inner life is not the same thing as being self-obsessed in the usual sense of wanting the world to notice us or get things our way. In fact, to not pay attention to one's own inner life is to neglect oneself, and lose contact with our selves. This is where our suffering stems from.

I found that once I got the hang of this inward looking I couldn't stop it. It was as if it had a momentum of its own. This doesn't mean that it happened automatically but that it became impossible to ignore the various afflictions that hit the Tess ego without simultaneously an impetus arising to look deeper into them. I became acutely aware of afflictions that I had usually glossed over to the point of not noticing them in the past. This was because I had learned to dismiss and suppress many thoughts and emotions as pragmatic in the business of getting on with daily life. We are taught this as children. We learn to put up with various ups and downs and learn that this is how life is for everyone. We learn to expect and accept suffering as part and parcel of the human condition. We are conditioned to dismiss what is not of value to the world and in the process we dismiss it to ourselves. We learn to fit in and get on with life without demanding unnecessary attention from others. Some of us learn this lesson better than others, but all of us have taken on some degree of conformity to those around us as a necessary aspect of survival in our family and community.

One way I became aware of these pervasive slights, the minor injuries to my sense of self, that I was in the habit of glossing over was from the sensations in the body. Often times, sensations that I recognized as anxiety, or some kind of defensiveness, arose and I did not know why they had arisen. I came to see that the sensations in the body are a trustworthy indicator of unconscious thoughts and feelings. With the understanding that sensations in the body (the sensations connected with emotional states) arise in response to some change, I could observe the sensation and then look for what had caused it. I found that slights I had learned to overlook were picked up on

89

by the body. It was a way of being able to notice afflictions to the ego that had in the past gone unnoticed.

On this retreat I also got the names of authors I had not heard of before: Nisargadatta, Ramana Maharshi, William Samuels, Adyashanti, and others. As I mentioned earlier, I had previously come across Douglas Harding but didn't get what he was writing about, really. This group TAT quoted freely from Christian, Buddhist, Sufi, Vedanta, poetry and so on. They respected and learned from all the traditions and yet were party to none. This reminded me of something I had read from *The Chasm of Fire*, by Irina Tweedie where she says her (Sufi) teacher told her: *"There are Muslim Sufis, there are Christian Sufis, there are Hindu Sufis."* And I'd add TAT Sufis!

I found there was something freeing about the fact that this group wasn't steeped in traditions and rituals and organization; they spoke in common language and yet were informed by the great traditions. I found this to be an extraordinary combination and one that appealed to me — a modern day version of The Perennial Wisdom.

The individuals present came from various backgrounds, including some long term Richard Rose students. Richard Rose had died only a few months prior to this retreat, and this was the first time they were meeting each other since his death. He had been living with Alzheimer's' for many years and had been in a nursing home. I was struck by the affection between them and their sorrow at his passing. It was a subtle thing because they didn't speak about it much. What was obvious was what a special role he had played in all their lives. So, even though I never met Richard Rose in the flesh, he has been one of the most profound influences in my life.

I returned home. I had travelled to the US many times and had a routine for how to deal with jet lag when I returned home. I'd get home around 8 or 9 in the morning, have breakfast, and go to bed for a few hours. Then I would get up in the afternoon and go to bed at the usual midnight hour. I'm a good sleeper so I never had trouble falling asleep on my return. This time however, I could not sleep. I tossed and turned and eventually got up after a few hours. I fully expected to sleep well when I got to bed that night but this did not happen. In fact, for the next three weeks or so I seemed to hardly sleep at all. I wasn't disturbed or upset in any conscious way, but still I couldn't sleep.

After three weeks I was walking from the kitchen to the hall door one day when a flare went up in my chest. Yes, I know that sounds odd, and it was very startling. It was as if a match had been lit just in front of my chest, in the heart area and immediately quenched. It was very quick but very definite. I wondered if I was having a stroke. I was observing myself carefully for the next few hours and everything seemed fine. Then it happened again. Then it started happening ten/twelve/twenty times a day. I had no idea what was going on but found that I was perfectly normal otherwise. Then after three weeks, one flash was followed by a heat wave. I recognized that menopause had arrived, suddenly and strangely. The heart flashes gradually died off over the next couple of weeks and the heat flushes took their place.

Menopause turned out to be quite difficult and strange for me. I became very light sensitive. I was frequently exhausted and spent hours lying on the couch, with sunglasses on. Nightmares and beauty dreams became more frequent, usually in short waves of maybe two or three nightmares one week and two or three beauty dreams some months later. While nightmares are full of fear and ugliness and hostility, what I call the beauty dreams were full of love and joy and beauty, of an order and quality I knew did not come from the world. Just as it was a relief to wake up from a nightmare, it was a disappointment to wake up from a beauty dream. The nightmares and beauty dreams had started about six or seven years earlier, if I remember correctly, but the frequency and intensity had now increased. I had always had, like most people I suppose, fearful and encouraging dreams, but the quality of these dreams now changed. For someone who had always paid attention to dreams, the symbolism was unmissable. I knew that something from the deep was coming up, that there was a change happening in me, and I reasoned that with all the observing and digging into the roots of mind this was to be expected. I also vaguely remembered having read about nightmares being part of the spiritual path, but I had not heard about what I called the beauty dreams. The dreams helped attune me to experiencing myself in a different way. I was changed by them, softened, humbled, surrendered, awed by the mystery that is life. I felt as if I was being given glimpses of what is real, what was beyond my usual perception.

During this time I had an ongoing experience, which I didn't understand then and still do not. Every night when I got into bed and closed my eyes, faces appeared. There were hordes of people walking from behind me, on my right hand side and some of them would turn and look directly into my face. They were mostly, if not all, women dressed in strange garb or clothes from foreign places and times. This would be so bright and alive that at times I had to check to see if my eyes were actually open or shut. This went on most nights for about a year and then it stopped happening. I mention it here because someone recently told me about this same thing happening to her.

I asked a Buddhist monk about it at the time and he said it was all my past lives being displayed to me. I can only think that we interpret things through whatever beliefs we hold and since I didn't then or now buy into the reincarnation belief, I still have no interpretation for this. But, for sure, something inner had come alive.

In November, two months after this retreat weekend, I was almost knocked over one day by what felt like I had been shot in the hip, the left one. The suddenness and severity left me lying on the couch for days, barely able to get up. I didn't know it then but with hindsight I can see that this was the beginning of a phase of unusual symptoms that lasted for almost five years. I made many trips to my doctor and had many tests performed, and they were always clear, but the ever changing symptoms persisted. I regularly Googled the current round of symptoms and what always came back was Kundalini and menopause. The symptoms moved across from the hip to the uterus area, then up the left side to the spleen area, then across to the stomach and up to the heart area and then up to the neck, face, and finally the head.

But, I'm jumping ahead of myself here. While I was at TAT I had been asked if I would like to participate in a women's online self-inquiry group. I did and for the next two years I communicated weekly with Anima Pundeer, who moderated the group, and a number of other women. This communication became a very significant part of my life. I was challenged in my beliefs, heard new ideas, and was inspired to continue with my spiritual search, as well as being delighted at having found friends on the path. It can be a very lonely path until one finds fellow seekers with whom one can communicate and share. I learned a lot in this group. I also had made contact with one of the TAT awakened men, Art Ticknor, who exchanged mails with me occasionally during this period. I didn't have any questions for him because I didn't know what I wanted to know, but the contact with him meant a lot to me. The fact that he would take the trouble to write to me was enough to make me take myself seriously, which was new for me.

The kind of ideas I was picking up on at this time was that I am not the ego; I am the observer. So, the challenge was how to become able to observe myself without getting lost in ego or reactions. This was no easy task, as became apparent over time. I knew that one way to recognize ego was as maintaining our image to the world. I could see that every time I put my foot in it, so to speak, or if I perceived that I was coming across in some situation as less than how I would like to be seen that there was an immediate, automatic reaction to correct the image. Again and again I observed this pattern happening, the perceived slight to ego and the automatic reaction. I observed the anxieties or irritation that arose and how they grabbed my total attention. This pattern was so strong and fast that I felt

94

that I would never be able to tolerate even the smallest slight without the defensive pattern arising. I could see what had happened immediately after the event and I could examine it but not while it was happening.

Once I had become aware of this pattern, its automaticity and its frequency, I could see for myself that what I was, in relation to others, was an automatic reactor. This was a new level of awareness. I could see all the ploys I used in the reactions: humor, distraction, discussion and so on. Ever since I was a child people used to say to me, "You talk too much." This was a really painful thing for me and of course the defenses around it were very high. I always reacted, right down to the soles of my feet, even if I didn't express it. This was my wound. It was the home feeding ground of my inner critic.

One day, after about a year of observing this reaction pattern, it happened that I was talking with someone, talking too much I judged, by some mild withdrawal from the person. I could see the reaction pattern arising, shutting up and changing the conversation to please the other, but I didn't go along with it. I simply watched the situation and the reaction pattern, even though there was a flood of anxiety. I continued on talking for some time and tolerated the anxiety without changing the behavior. I continued to be annoying while I watched the irritation of my friend. Something in me changed in those moments and I knew it. I had become able to observe myself without giving in to the demands of ego. I had become able to tolerate a less than perfect image of myself. I knew it was a milestone of some kind and I was pleased that all this effort to observe myself was indeed working. I could see that inner discipline was developing. This was the beginnings of becoming The Observer or The Witness as it is sometimes referred to.

The Observer had become as strong, or stronger, than the ego, at least in some moments. This was also the beginning of detachment from my personality.

The ox was becoming tamer.

Around this time also I had been doing what is known as Inner Child work— making efforts to reconnect with my natural spontaneous self. One day while meditating, or looking around inside the psyche I noticed something move. I was startled. This was like a bundle of energy, to the right hand side towards the back which moved, where I had never expected anything to move by itself. I investigated and found a little girl, maybe about four or five years old, shy, neglected and abandoned. I recognized it as my inner child. I followed this up with making conscious contact with this inner aspect of myself, talking to my child, re-incorporating aspects of her (myself) that I had abandoned in favor of being a responsible adult. Something in me was freed up. I became more spontaneous and appreciative of fun and play. I had recovered a lost part of myself.

Early in 2007 I was living in Armenia for four months as a long-term election observer. Armenia is where George Gurdjieff, founder of The Fourth Way School, had been born. As you might recall, Gurdjieff had been one of my earliest influences on this path, and I was familiar with his main practice which he called Self- Remembering. I decided to do Self-Remembering "all the time" while in Armenia and I did put tremendous effort into doing this practice during my time there. I had lots of opportunities to do this because I was often travelling with people who spoke only Armenian so I couldn't participate in the conversations. I took advantage of the situation. I had taken one book with me on that trip: *I Am That*, by Nisargadatta. I read a page every morning and made it my topic of the day.

In summer of 2007 I attended The Douglas Harding gathering in Salisbury in England. Harding taught a practice called "Seeing." From the first hour I found I could "See" constantly and easily because what I had been doing as Self-Remembering was the same thing. It was a subtle shift in perception, so subtle and natural that it was easy to miss. Being with the Harding group for a weekend consolidated the practice. From that time on I was able to do it (See) consciously at any time or place. This was the state I was in when I made a second visit to TAT in September 2007.

The Ox is no meek lamb, and the Herdsman, no good shepherd. Only a tough Herdsman can deal with a strong-willed bull. God knows just what will happen when He brands the bull with the Seal of his image, yet only this can seal the Ox to Him forever as His own possession. This Seal, of course, will burn the bull to the depths of his being, burn a Centre right through him, and it will be painful. At the onset of this ordeal, however, a film-like veil is put over his mind, a veil through which, in time, God can be seen everywhere, a depth of vision that never leaves – though initially it all but blinds the Ox. Following this, the moment He looks inward to his familiar Centre, instead of light, there is a bottomless black hole, the sight of which begins the painful burning through to the depths of his existence. Now there is a fire in the belly and the bull goes wild. First on his agenda is never to look "within" again – but how can this be avoided? Finally, screwing up his courage he decided to "face it," to deliberately look down into this

dark pit even if it kills him – it might be better to be dead anyway. But lo and behold, looking down there is God's Big Eye looking back at him! What a shock! But now he knows the direction: go down into that pit where, at bottom God Is. So he makes this journey through a revolting self to his bottommost existence – a point where one can go no further and where one eventually finds a peace that surpasses definition. This sacred space, the peace of God, becomes a refuge from a self still storming wildly about and above us. We hang on to this peace for dear life until, finally, the storm gradually subsides and the Centre becomes bright, rises to the top and is ever available. Where we thought God was out to break our spirit, it turns out God gives us His Spirit instead, this is the way it goes. Then comes the certifying revelation of an abiding, permanent oneness of the two, and with that, a whole new person (Ox) appears. (Bernadette Roberts – Taming the Ox)

SEEING THE BENEFITS OF THE INNER STRUGGLE

6. Riding the Ox Home

Mounting the ox, slowly I return homeward.
The voice of my flute intones through the evening.
Measuring with hand-beats the pulsating harmony,
I direct the endless rhythm.
Whoever hears this melody will join me.

The sixth picture suggests the tranquility and joy that reunion with the source of existence brings; now the oxherd rides on the back of the ox, joyously playing his flute. The verse suggests that he has been freed from old fears and anxieties and that so freed, he can now express his creative energies in celebration of life. (John Koller)

In September 2007 I went back to the TAT intensive weekend. It was followed by a women's retreat led by Anima Pundeer, the woman who moderated the women's online dialogue group. These were the women I had been corresponding with over the past two years. I was truly excited to meet them in person and get to know them. I considered them to be my best friends on the planet, the ones who knew me in my truest form. By the time I left the retreat I felt that my friendship with each of them had been cemented securely, despite the fact that in the final feedback session all of them told me they had no feedback to give me. It seemed like they didn't understand me. I was really upset. They found me baffling, it seemed. I couldn't understand it.

One thing did happen during the women's retreat which somehow gave me a hint of what was happening to me. I had found the abandoned skin shed by a molting snake just outside my bedroom window in the cabin we were staying. I am afraid of snakes and this meant that danger lurked very close by. Yet, I felt that there was something striking about finding the skin of a creature that had outgrown it. I did feel there was special significance to me finding this, and not any of the other women who were present, and outside my window. I was aware that in nature there follows a period of danger and vulnerability between a creature growing out of its old skin and growing into a new one. I felt this was happening to me. "Perhaps," I thought, "this is what is happening to me and this is why the women are not able to give me feedback." I didn't know anything for sure and didn't feel any different from my normal self but I had hints that something was happening and that these changes were more obvious to others than to me. I did feel vulnerable. By the time I left the retreat I felt that something like my inner skin had dissolved. I felt naked inwardly.

I went to Trinidad and Tobago immediately from that retreat because my sister was getting married there. There I spent several days alone, on the beach, or resting in the house from the sun while the wedding folk were busy with arrangements. One morning when I was walking the streets of Port-of-Spain, suddenly, an enormous energy arrived from behind me on my right side. It descended upon me like a sudden tornado and I got a terrible fright. It was enormous. I inwardly shrieked, "Who are you? What do you want?" Amazingly, "She" responded, because it was a feminine energy, not in words but directly. Later I came to call this "voice" Universal Mother (UM).

The first thing she did was flash to me, inwardly, the exact image that had come into my mind the day I had almost committed suicide around thirty years earlier, and with it came the knowledge that she had been with me every step of the way. For all the hardships and troubles I had lived during the intervening years, she had been watching over me and been with me all the time. She also showed gratitude to me for having taken on this path, not having committed suicide and for having struggled to do the best I could. I felt weak at the knees with this knowledge. She also let me know that the worst was over but that there was still a ways to go, and she would be with me through the challenges I had yet to face. She became a soothing, guiding voice that obviously knew me better than I knew myself. While this energy or presence or voice was felt as a protective presence, as I mentioned above, I understood that I had to undergo various experiences that would be difficult and challenging but that she would protect me during these times. The image by which this knowledge was given to me was of a mother allowing, encouraging, her child to learn to walk, but not at the edge of The Grand Canyon.

With this first visit came a "download" of knowledge that corrected some of my wrong assumptions and understandings. One such misunderstanding that I held was that there are spiritual people and non-spiritual people. I had thought that people who talk about and do spiritual practices were spiritual and the rest were not. I was shown that there are only spiritual people. All are "children of god" or creations of the one source. The download corrected this error, automatically, it seemed. I was not even aware that I had this assumption running until this experience. I can say that this correction changed my view of humanity. It re-arranged how I saw others and how I understood what is happening here in the relative world. From this time on Universal Mother guided me. She became my dearest friend. I understood this to be the voice of intuition—the inner teacher. Over time it became that the division between UM and me melted away. It happened that I was no longer I; I was a We. I was not other than Universal Mother and Universal Mother was not other than me. Riding the ox home had now begun. For some reason I found it difficult to tell anyone about this "event." Somehow it was "secret" between me and this voice of intuition. I knew her as an actual experiential energy within myself.

By the end of September I was back in Ireland, and life, it seemed was simply rolling along as usual, except that I had this inner grace. A new level of equanimity emerged. I felt solid and calm. There was a new level of inward vigilance, waiting for visits from Universal Mother. She did not come at my beck and call but arrived unannounced and unexpectedly.

Within the month, the usual weekly online report (AR) arrived and I set about responding to it as usual. What I refer to as the online report is a group moderated by TAT teacher Anima Pundeer, whereby we had weekly email exchange on topics pertaining to spiritual seeking. One week Anima and we, about six to eight of us, posed questions to each other and responded the following week. I now moderate such a group myself.

Every time I tried to write something for that week, I simply could not do it. This went on day after day and the something that was inhibiting me from writing became stronger and stronger. I was torn apart. Rationally, I was sure that it was a good thing to be participating in this group with my new-found level of friendship with my women friends, but intuition had another idea. Intuition was preventing me from writing. By the end of the week I succumbed to intuition and left the group.

Immediately upon making this difficult decision a flood of relief came over me. It was obvious that this was the right "decision." I was totally baffled by this at the time but over time I came to recognize that one of the ways intuition worked for me was by this "preventing" energy.

By now Art and I were corresponding regularly, getting to know each other and I was coming to rely on him. Intuition told me that I could rely on him and that he would not lead me astray. This came about when one day I asked Intuition (UM) who I should listen to most, Her or Art. I felt there might be a conflict. I was immediately presented with a vision of a violin being presented to someone along with the question—if you gave a violin to someone for a present, what would you want them to do with it? The thoughts that followed were something like this: "I wouldn't want them to use it for decorative pur-poses – hanging it on a wall to show everyone that they had it; I wouldn't want them telling everyone about it but not using it. I'd want them to make every effort to use it for the purpose it was made for. Just use it, practice it and skill and knowledge will develop." I knew that UM was telling me that she was giving me Art as a great gift and it was up to me to use it. There never was any conflict between the inner voice and my beloved human helper. In fact, they worked together.

Around November time I had a dream in which I was standing above an enormous beach of white sand with million, billions, trillions, countless grains of sand when I noticed that one grain seemed unusual. I went down to see what it was, and it turned out to be a golden egg the size of the grain of sand, and that egg was me. The universe was hatching me. I knew this was a significant dream. The following day UM came when I was wondering about what this could mean and let me know that from now on this process was out of my hands. I interpreted it as: once a woman becomes pregnant, the pregnancy proceeds according to its own program, and it is not in the hands of the mother, so to speak. All I had to or could do from now on was to facilitate the process as best I could.

Over the next few days—and there had been a lot of these conversations going on—I was rendered surrendered. This happened suddenly. All goals or desires simply vanished in favor of what was to come. I didn't do this. I couldn't have done this. It happened and I was filled with gratitude for this grace. I used to ask intuition questions and sometimes get answers and sometimes I was met with silence. I took this to mean, enough for now! That day I asked, "How long does this universal pregnancy take?" Silence! Shortly afterwards the number 33 kept coming into my mind, large and persistent. I thought that must mean 33 years, so it must mean that the final realization will happen on my death bed. Many years later, on checking back it turned that it happened exactly 33 months later. But by now, my mind had slowed down and wasn't much interested in dwelling on such questions for long. Acceptance of whatever was to come had arrived. I'll just mention here that once these "strange" things began to happen to me, I remembered books I had long ago read on the lives of the saints, which at the time made no sense to me, but now I was comforted by having read them. I now understood what they had been writing about and could accept that I was not going crazy. This is a universal condition or possibility. But it was startling to find that this was happening to me. It was completely unexpected.

By the following January or so, a crisis had arrived in my life, from a most unexpected quarter. I had had a row with one of my sisters. We are a family who get on well together and keep our distance from each other in what I think is a healthy way. But, one of my sisters had made some unacceptable accusations against me about two years earlier. I had avoided much contact with her after that because this was how we dealt with things in our family, but now it was decided that all the sisters, seven of us, would go away together for a weekend. First off I agreed but then intuition intervened and said "No!" I had to deal with the situation honestly and not act one way while I felt or thought another way. I let my sisters know that I would not be joining them because of the things that one sister had said. This caused a lot of upset in the sisters. It ended up with my sister who had made the accusations and me going to therapy or mediation together. This brought out a lot of stuff from childhood and family issues and in the process I had to come clean with myself, more than anyone, about issues I had not dealt with or previously recognized. One issue that I became aware of was that as "the scapegoat" in the family; I was the carrier of the negative emotions or as Jung would have termed it "the shadow." This sister had articulated the family shadow. She said things like, "Everyone knows you are a liar. Nobody trusts you. Nobody has any respect or time for you." Devastating and all as this was, I was absolutely sure that this was projection and I had plenty of evidence from other aspects of my life that this was not how I was seen outside of the family. My years of therapy were paying off, and at the same time, while this was happening I felt as if something bigger was unfolding. As much as I wanted to belong in my family, I felt that even if I was rejected by everyone, I could bear it. I could bear it in favor of the greater unfolding that I knew was underway, even though I had no idea what it might entail. An inner courage had arisen from "god knows where," as the phrase goes. My sister and I worked through what we needed to and were able to continue our lives in sisterly friendship afterwards.

One of the elements of this incident was that my mother had died a few years earlier, and I realized that while she was alive I always played the role of not confronting the confronter for the sake of "family peace." I had learned non-confrontation from her. It was only after she had gone that I could change that behavior and that I could replace it with authenticity and honesty and learn to stand up for myself in the face of unacceptable behavior within the family. I had already learned this in other aspects of my life. I had long before recognized that there was an unwritten rule in our family which might have been termed: "the keep Mammy happy rule" in therapeutic circles. Every family and society has tacit rules and learning to break through them takes courage and the drive for authenticity or integrity. Becoming true to oneself inevitably leads to the need to question the beliefs and assumptions and motivations that we learned in our families. I could no longer play the role of scapegoat in my family.

While the ideas we learn in our families and society are a necessary tool kit with which to start out our lives as independent individuals, they are also limiting and distract us from our core being. These are the ideas that cut us off from our true inner selves. It takes courage and determination to look at our conditioning, which includes the tacit agreements that operate in families and societies. This courage or determination usually comes when someone finds their suffering intolerable. They become aware that they are riddled with inner conflicts, feel stressed and anxious all the time, wondering what life is all about and finding it hard to go on living life in the same way one had lived it up to now. This state is also often accompanied by feeling that there must be something more to life than mere survival. There is! Being willing to face our inner conflicts, which often show up as outer conflicts, is the path of returning to integrity and authenticity—to wholeness and ultimately to self-knowledge. Spiritual maturation or maturing into spirit is all about becoming authentic to ourselves, recovering our natural essence from the overlay of conditioning taken on while growing up.

The mediation ended up very well and was brought to a sudden end when my husband became ill. Shortly afterwards he was diagnosed with leukemia and thus began the next six years of caring for him and all the issues that arise in such circumstances, but particularly the specter of death having entered our house. For about eighteen months, I forgot all about spiritual work, or thought I did, except that Art wrote to me regularly. That was a great comfort. My memory is that most of the letters were chatty and friendly and encouraging and always one or two remarks or sentences that stopped me in my tracks. It was as if he knew what I was thinking, and understood my state of mind better than I did myself. I had dreams but mostly my only practice was to quickly pray, "Help me to accept Thy Will"... every night as I got into bed. There were many nights I came home from the hospital knowing that Seamus might not make it through the night.

In one dream during this time, I was walking down the street of some unknown town with a great friend. We knew each other intimately and loved each other dearly for a very long time. When we got to the end of the street I turned to him and said, " I know you so well, my dearest friend, but I can't remember who you are." At that he morphed into Jesus and let me know that if I were a Buddhist he would have appeared to me as Buddha. Jesus was my friend, the friend of friends! I awoke startled, full of love and joy at having rediscovered my friend. I was amazed by this dream because I had turned my back on Catholicism when I was around nineteen and not paid any heed to Jesus since then. Once again, I recognized this as a significant dream.

From then on many of the teachings I had learned as a child came back to me. I would find myself remembering them throughout the day. But I now understood them in a mature way. It was not the only visit I had from Jesus, and I was made to understand that dreams and intuitions which had Jesus in them were simply using images or symbols that were familiar to me and that if I had been from a different culture, the appropriate symbols from that culture would be used. I took it to mean that certain energies get interpreted or translated into language based on the symbolism in the individual. Universal symbols are translated into meaning in the personal context.

Shortly after Seamus became ill, we had to have a downstairs bedroom built for him. His health was so fragile that it was not at all clear that he would ever come home from hospital to occupy his proposed new bedroom. The night before I needed to sign a contract with the builders for a lot of money, I was thinking about whether or not to go ahead with it. Intuition came to me and said "Death will come at 61." This answered my question, Seamus would not be 61 for another six weeks or so, so I should sign the contract and get the building work started. Seamus turned 61, and came home and turned 62 and was doing quite well, so I wondered about my intuition or my interpretation of it. Maybe I was going to die at 61 myself or maybe our dog would die when one of us was 61. I knew the intuition was vague, but it definitely said that death would arrive at 61. And by now, I knew intuition never lied, only that I didn't always interpret it correctly.

About eighteen months after Seamus became ill, he was home, doing very well, and I suddenly remembered that I hadn't meditated for a very long time. I went upstairs and sat to meditate. I immediately descended into the deepest meditative state I had ever experienced. About ten minutes later Seamus called me. I got up immediately and was straight back in the world. I was amazed by this. Something had obviously happened over the past couple of years, completely below the level of conscious awareness.

Often on waking in the morning some thought seemed to have arisen during the night. I assumed it was what had been going on in a forgotten dream or maybe the theme of a dream. One morning I awoke to the thought of pride, which was something I had been trying to identify in myself ever since Art had said something about it to me in 2007. I was trying to see in what ways I was prideful in relation to God or what had created me. Another way of saying this is that I was trying to see in what subtle ways I, ego, was taking credit for or control of things for which I was not responsible or had control over. I suddenly realized that my sense of responsibility in taking

111

care of Seamus was nothing short of pride, arrogance in relation to the source of my being. God, "what is," was taking care
of Seamus, not me. And at the same time it was obvious that
taking responsibility in so far as I could was right action and in
alignment with spiritual development.

    With this realization came a wave of shame at my ar-
rogance which was followed by a new level of humility. Somewhere in Christian literature I had read something along the
lines of: what gifts can we give God who has given us everything? The article said that our gifts take the form of doing what
is asked of us, such as taking responsibility for the care of a sick
person, patience in wanting results for our efforts, kindness
to others even when they are not kind to us and so on. This is
done in the understanding that we are trying to facilitate an inner transformation in ourselves, the shift from our false floating
identities to our one true identification as consciousness. I feel
the need to explain this because I find that some modern teachings deny the value of developing virtues or ethical lifestyle
on the basis that anything we decide to adopt is just another
version of ego. There is truth to this, but my experience shows
that having adopted "virtues" they are then taken from us when
no longer needed. Adopting an ethical lifestyle is a stepping
stone, a necessary or at least helpful step in the dissolution of
ego. A "virtuous" lifestyle is alignment with "what is," an aid to
undoing our inbuilt arrogance in relation to our source. What I
am trying to point out here is that the self-serving nature of ego
is in contradiction to our true selves. This is not about external
acts but about becoming able to see how ego functions and how
that process interferes with us becoming our true natural selves.

Realizing that I was not responsible for taking care of Seamus in no way affected my taking care of him. I continued doing what I had been doing but with a different understanding of what was happening. Seamus had been given the role of sickness; I had been given the role of caretaker, as part of our journey to wisdom and transformation. We were puppets being played.

Around this time I was given a present of a five day stay at a retreat center in an isolated hermitage on the grounds of the retreat center. It was by way of giving me a break from caring, a rest. I had begun to think about getting into a meditation group. I felt the need to be in the company of others who were spiritual seekers. I went to a group nearby and met a woman I had not met before. She and I were the only women present. After the session I asked her if she knew of any group that had more women in it. She told me that her sister was a satsang teacher and would be giving satsang in Galway the following weekend. I had never heard of satsang but determined to go anyway. I did. It was Jac O'Keeffe. This was the first time I had come across a group of spiritual seekers in Ireland. I heard some things from Jac that made a lot of sense to me and confirmed what was going on with me. A week later Stuart Swartz was in Galway and I went to see him also. Again, he was saying things that confirmed for me that there was a transformation taking place in me, although I used different language.

A week later, towards the end of 2009, I went on solitary retreat. From the start of it I found myself falling into silence, or rather the world was falling silent and yet somehow in this silence I heard everything clearly: the birds singing, the beetles scratching around, the leaves moving in the wind and so on.

113

This silence would come for maybe ten or fifteen minutes and then back to the normal noisiness of the world. It was as if the usual static on the radio cleared up for a time and then returned. This Silence, I knew it was something special, always present but blocked out by the inner static. For the first time I felt I understood what the word "silence" meant.

When I had been to TAT in 2007, Art had said to me that I should take another look at pride. I had tried to deal with my pride over the years but it seemed obvious that he saw something of pride in me that I couldn't see in myself. After that I looked hard for pride and found a lower level of pride, or ego, simply another word for the same thing. I had done what I could with it each time and learned to change my attitudes in relation to what I found.

A couple of nights into this retreat I was once again thinking about pride and feeling totally unable to get to the root of it. I was now aware of my arrogance in relation to what created me. I realized that I couldn't do anything about my sense of existence and that my sense of existence was at the root of this pride. I was ashamed of it, of myself but couldn't do anything about it, I felt sure. I was overcome with desperation and a sense of despair. I begged whatever there is to relieve me of this terrible affliction, the affliction of myself. I knew absolutely that I couldn't do it myself. I felt frustrated and despairing and hopelessly inadequate in my efforts to deal with pride, the pride of feeling that I existed. I recognized that getting to the root of my own sense of existence was beyond anything that I could do. I felt that I did not even know what it was that I was trying to do. What was I even doing here, sitting alone in a cabin struggling with a problem I did not comprehend and couldn't do anything about? These were the kinds of thoughts and feelings going on in me at that moment.

Shortly afterwards I got an awful pain in my chest. First I thought, "Oh no, I'm going to have a terrible attack of indigestion." This was something that rarely happened, and it was so inconvenient to have it now and here where I could not get a remedy. This pain became so bad that I thought "I'm having a heart attack. This is the end." At that moment something reached into my chest and whipped the whole thing out. It was as if a tree had started growing in my chest, was getting bigger and bigger and was about to kill me when suddenly this "hand" tore the entire thing out, roots and all. The event must have taken only minutes but the intensity of it shocked and frightened me, and then just as suddenly released me.

I was sitting by the fire, staring into the flames and wondering about this event for some time. Then as I got up to go to the toilet a vision appeared before me. In the vision, what appeared was a mountain made of layers. The mountain started a little distance out from me, and the first layer, on ground level was my family. The next layer was the community I grew up in. I recognized individuals long since dead. The next layer was everyone I had ever gone to school with. Each layer was further distant and more crowded and on they went up to the top of the mountain which was crowded with everyone who had ever served me in any way in all the places I had lived or visited in my years of travel. There was a layer somewhere around the middle which contained all the authors and spiritual teachers I had been influenced by. It included Shakespeare, Jesus, The Buddha, and many, many more. Right at the front, my immediate family was on the left and to the right was a blank area.

115

During this vision I was conversing with WHOMEVER. I didn't recognize it as Universal Mother, but certainly an inner "voice" that was answering my questions, mainly "who is that?" When I asked who or what was in the blank area I got "TAT types" and with that the vision faded.

What was amazing during this vision was that "I" had disappeared. I was a blank, maybe a blank consciousness. I wasn't there. It seemed like the entire world, my world, was there, but no "me." And yet, questions were asked and answered. The best I can describe this is to call it direct mind to mind communication. I don't think that words were necessary or used during this time. Words were not necessary.

It all seemed very clear and simple during the vision but afterwards I tried to understand what it meant, what it signified. "Each one's world is the world of the individual" was the interpretation of the vision I came up with. But, the mind was so confused or shocked by this idea that it couldn't take it in at the time. What I was left with was the knowing that the world is ethereal, without substance, a dream, a projection. The big question was: "whose dream?"… since I was gone, or didn't exist, never had, it seemed" Who dreams the dream of the world? Who dreams the dream of me? If I was not there, then who or what is dreaming me? The feeling I was left with over the coming months was that I knew what I was not, but I did not know what I am. At this time my mind had become very slow and wasn't much interested in trying to interpret the vision any further. There was a great sense of acceptance of everything, without the need to understand. Following this experience you could say I was left in a state of "limbo"—a state of not knowing, and not needing to know. This "knowing /not knowing" was more a state of living without any identity. The habitual identities that I had lived with all my life had disappeared in terms of having any power or authority to back them up. The underlying assumptions that: I am a body, I am a mind, I am a doer, I am the experiencer, etc., had collapsed. Life became simply the present moment, without questions. All or most intellectual activity had died away.

What followed was months in which my mind operated on automatic, it seemed. Daily functioning continued as normal against a backdrop of simplicity and docility and not knowing. The night following this vision there was a huge storm, with rain and wind. I awoke to find that I was the rain and the wind. I was the storm. I lay in bed for hours as the storm. It was obvious that something major had happened, but I could not figure what it was. I must have had some ideas about people becoming unable to function as a result of such experiences because I was wondering if I would be able to drive home safely the next day.

I fell back to sleep early in the morning for a few hours, and when I awoke later I had returned to being myself, in a way. I knew I was back to being able to cope and live normally, and I knew that I had been radically changed by the experience, but I had no idea what that change might entail. I had not been able to understand this experience until after the final realization which happened nine months later, when I became able to see it as a milestone on the path to awakening. This experience was a fatal blow to ego/self. The sense of self, of my existence, that I had begged to be taken from me, was taken away.

I stopped into a cafe on the way home next day, as much as anything, to see if I looked and acted normal to the general public. Nobody paid a blind bit of attention to me and that was a relief. After getting home I wrote to Art telling him that the end had come. I now knew my true nature. I did not exist; I was not. After all, was this not what the satsang people had said only a week before? This must be what they meant, I thought.

That night I had a dream in which I saw the golden egg again. I knew it as the same golden egg of previous dreams but there was something different. The golden egg was now huge and there was a crack in it. Inside the egg was me, the "me" that was undergoing the spiritual pregnancy. The fact that I could be shown this process in progress and know that I knew that the "me" that appeared to be undergoing the process was not the "me" who could witness it did leave me with a paradox, but I was in such a place of acceptance that I could not think about it. I knew there couldn't be two of me, and hadn't I just been shown that I didn't exist? My mind "stopped" when this paradox was noticed. As I had been rendered docile in a way that I cannot explain, I simply awaited whatever would happen next, not knowing and fully accepting whatever might ensue. I had been rendered not knowing and not needing to know. I was in the "hands of the gods," childlike, trusting, vigilant, grounded, and calmly anticipating.

The experience/vision with the cracked egg let me know that the chick had not yet been fully hatched. Don't forget that I am a child who grew up on a farm so an image such as this has an immediate and intimate and obvious interpretation for me. The intimacy of the symbolism in dreams at this time was extraordinary. The docility was so complete that there was no hint of desire for the end. The feeling was that if this took the rest of my life, then so be it. Writing this now, years later, it seems that it would have been natural to desire the end, considering that I understood what was happening, but the state itself did not permit any desire. I had no idea how long it takes for a "universal egg" to hatch. It would all happen according to its own laws and it was none of my business. I was not even interested except as an observer of the process. That was my mindset at this time.

The next morning there was mail from Art. I hesitated before I opened it. Even though I had written to him saying the final denouement had come only yesterday, I now knew this was not it. He wrote, "That is a major milestone on the path, but it is not IT." So, Art and intuition were in agreement! There was more to go. So be it! It took me some time to notice that Universal Mother had gone too.

Riding Home

Who goes home is a "branded" new Ox – the old one is dead. And here begins a whole new life, a life "I" no longer live, but "We" live. The Ox can no more be aware of himself than he is of the other half – God. The two are one in knowing and willing. With a fearless freedom and a divine Centre of imperturbable peace and joy, they set out and return to the marketplace whence they came. The marketplace, however, is but a testing ground, a challenge to the imperturbable Centre into which everything that touches self (Ox) ultimately disappears. Making their way through the marketplace the divine Centre imperceptibly expands as every aspect of the self that can arise disappears into It never to be experienced again. Thus the divine Centre expands in proportion as self (Ox) disappears - "He must increase, I must decrease," the saying goes. The Rider does not lead the Ox – no reins needed – because the Ox comes to know the Rider's mind so well he can anticipate Its will and direction – usually the hardest. And so the two, Ox and Herdsman, bull their way through the ups and downs of life, always landing on their feet. Then there comes a time when nothing can touch the Ox at all, there being nothing left to touch – self has been lived through completely, there is nothing left to experience. Now this has all been a good and adventurous life, a great life that God intends everyone to live in oneness with Him. Here nothing is wanting, nothing left to be achieved, no further to go in this life. From here on we can only head for our eternal, heavenly home. (Bernadette Roberts – Riding Home)

A Profound Shift in Perspective Occurs

7. Ox Vanishes – Herdsman Remains

Astride the ox, I reach home.
I am serene. The ox too can rest.
The dawn has come.
In blissful repose, Within my thatched dwelling
I have abandoned the whip and ropes

In the seventh picture the oxherd has realized his identity with the ox; the ox can be forgotten, for it is none other than the experience of everyday things. This can be interpreted to mean that the separation of practice and realization has been overcome, as has the separation of ordinary reality and the ultimate reality. Until now he has been practicing meditation as a means of achieving enlightenment. But with realization of the non-duality of existence comes awareness of the identity of means and ends; practice itself is realization. (John Koller)

Back home—I found that inside I was dead, or so it felt like; but on the outside I was the same, cheerful and chatty as ever. The experience of the vision had confirmed for me what I had known for a good while, that indeed the spiritual fruition was proceeding. I was deeply happy about this. This was all I really cared about. All I wanted was to not interfere with it and to continue doing whatever facilitated this fruition. I wasn't able to think about what had happened. I was in a state of not knowing and this was accompanied by a deep state of acceptance. I trusted that it would work out fine in its own time. It was interesting to see that the aspect of my mind that dealt with issues of daily life functioned fine. I read very little. When I picked up a book, I read no more than a couple of sentences at a time. Art

Ticknor, my teacher, published his first book during this time and I couldn't read it. All I could read were a few sentences here and there. This really brought home to me how little I was able to take in at this time. It was obvious to me that I was in a very different state from how I had been in the past, the one who devoured books.

I was neither happy nor unhappy, effortful or effortless. Externally life rolled along with all the usual caring duties, visitors, housework, and the like. But, I was in a kind of no-man's land.

It was obvious that something profound had changed, but I wasn't able to articulate what it was, not even to myself. It was as if part of my mind had gone to sleep: no imagination, no running thought streams, no unnecessary mental activity. It was something like moving around in a kind of fog where I could see perfectly on the outside but nothing on the inside. Considering I had always had such a busy mind, this certainly felt different. All imagination and fantasy creating had gone. It felt as if creativity had left and as someone who had always had a creative mind, this was a striking contrast. I was in a state that was undisturbable, unexcitable, and grounded.

I mentioned earlier about Kundalini and the movement of subtle energies in the body. From this time on there was a lot of subtle energy activity in and around the head. There were no headaches or discomfort of any kind, but I spent hours every day, in between my household duties, seated, looking at this constant subtle energy movement in the head—pushing, expanding, stretching, lifting, flowing, solidifying, dissolving, etc. It dominated my attention when mundane activities did not require it. In the four years since my first trip to TAT in 2005, I had been experiencing a lot of energies in or around the body. I recognized them as subtle energies and understood them as Kundalini energy as described in Indian literature. The energy movements in the head were of this kind. These energy movements had over the four years moved up the body from the pelvic area to the head. Since I was accustomed to these energy movements I was not concerned by them and understood this phenomenon as an aspect of the process that was taking place in me.

One day, several months after this experience, a friend asked me how I was. She wanted to invite me to a concert. She was concerned about how I was coping with the ongoing challenges of fulltime caring and frequent crises arising in my daily life. I started to tell her how accepting and "neutral" I felt and that I was uninterested in getting involved in social activities. I told her I was simply not interested in any social activities. She said that everything I said sounded like I was in a deep depression. I knew I wasn't depressed. I wasn't feeling depressed—just not interested in the world. I was completely incapable of making plans for future activities. I was so grounded in the present that any idea of past or future was beyond what I could think about. I simply lived in the present and responded to whatever came up. I knew this wasn't depression, at least not in the way it is usually meant. I knew this was a different kind of state from anything I had experienced before. I quickly retreated from telling her any more, realizing how it all sounded. How could I tell her that for me there was no future, no past, only now. The mind could dwell in the present only. All introspection and imagination were gone during the day. But dreams were bringing up stuff—not pleasant things either. There was simply "this" with no questions, as if the mind had been numbed and this was all accompanied by an unshakable equanimity.

This was a state of no qualities so to speak, no excitement, no depression, no anticipation, no regrets, no planning, no happiness, no unhappiness, no imagination. No wonder it sounded like what is usually termed depression, but I was absolutely sure that I was not depressed, only somehow numb to the world, in the arms of something I did not know but knew it to be. There was total passivity but it was not a depressed passivity. It was an active passivity. There was the palpable sense of something going on; a process was playing itself out and it had nothing to do with me, even though I was at the center of it. This inner stability and calmness that I could not describe was accompanied by a sense of readiness and mild anticipation. It was more than having been rendered surrendered; it was the outcome of that rendering. As the inner mind was asleep at this time, I didn't have any interest in analyzing it.

It was in trying to describe my condition to my friend that I became aware of the profundity of the change that had come over me. It was as if a veil had come between me and the world, a veil that shut me off from the world while at the same time making it very clear. The show went on relentlessly, but it couldn't touch me. There were regular crises in my own household as Seamus' illness was the kind of illness that generated crises. I could see this unshakable equanimity and steadiness in myself as I dealt with these situations.

During this period an image came to me. I don't know whether it appeared as I awoke from a dream in the morning or if a mental image formed during the day. This is, and was, a way

126

that spiritual knowledge was often presented to me. The image was of the whole human world comprising of spinning tops. The tops came in all sizes, some spinning fast and some slowly, but mostly spinning in a clockwise direction. A small percentage were spinning in a counterclockwise direction and a very few were not spinning at all, but sitting perfectly balanced and stable in the midst of all the spinning. The tops were bumping into each other and this was upsetting to the tops. Large fast spinning tops were causing a lot of disruption and the stable balanced tops caused a slowing down or stabilizing effect on the tops nearby. The clarity and simplicity of this image described the world as it was for me, at that time. I understood myself to be one of the non-spinning tops.

During this phase also there was a recurring dream theme which had first begun to appear a couple of years earlier. The theme of the dream was that I was wandering the world looking for a place to rest, a safe place to rest my head but could find none. Jesus said, "Foxes have dens and birds have nests, but the Son of Man has no place to lay his head"(Luke Gospel 9.58). I didn't think of what Jesus had said then, but this is a precise description of the feeling and my interpretation of those dreams. In my journal of March 2010 I have written, "I am always alone, no one to help me, but there are people who want to hunt and catch me. I have no rights—not even a place to lay my head—no security, no safety, no support. Who is this 'I' who is so abandoned and worthless?"

Around this time I went to a weekend satsang with Jac O'Keefe. She said something along the lines that there is a phase when the conditioning is no longer functioning, but it takes time for it all to get burned out. I wondered if this was what was happening to me. I had been rendered "perfectly passive," to borrow a phrase from Bernadette Roberts: "To be perfectly passive—to belong perfectly to God—is the most difficult of human accomplishments." The egg had cracked but the shell had not yet fully fallen off; the birth had not yet happened. The Ox had vanished and the herdsman remained.

During this time I also became aware of many psychic phenomena happening around me and in our house. Many times somebody I had not thought of for years entered my mind and the next moment they would be at the door. Seamus and I would start talking about someone at the same moment, people neither of us had thought about for years. I became used to this kind of thing happening and learned to be reticent about sharing. I noticed that others thought me strange, as if I had some psychic power, when something like this came out. These incidents confirmed for me the ephemeral nature of the world. It was as if I had to get used to this idea. My mind still wanted to view the world as a physical reality but these incidents reminded me of what the vision had shown me. The psychic incidents and startling synchronicities that occurred during this time loosened my hold on my previous understanding of what the world is. It was as if I was being given time to adapt to the new understanding. My mind couldn't take in what had been shown in the vision experience all in one go; it needed time to make the shift. I felt that I was being adjusted.

Universal Mother had vanished. I had no structure to hold on to, no sense of a me, nothing to hold on to and yet, I was totally calm, grounded and experiencing equanimity. I lived my days by putting one foot in front of the other and responding to what came up with no thoughts about it much. I wasn't able to think. The mind had been numbed. After about five or six months of being in this state, I began to develop a longing to be alone in some safe place for some extended time. This desire arose from the depths of me, the first desire to arise in months. It was surprising in its insistence and felt intensely after the months of emotional deadness. It felt like the desire to create a space in which to go into labor. I set about arranging for a solitary retreat. It took a few months to be able to find a week when Seamus did not have medical appointments and find someone who was able to take care of him at home. I simply trusted and felt confident that no crisis would arise during my proposed retreat.

One morning during this phase I awoke to know that TAT was no longer useful to me. All my props were being taken from me—even props I had not realized had become props along the way. I was upset and surprised, but the message was very clear that I was now finished with TAT. Even though I refer to Art as my teacher, I had always felt that the whole TAT group was my teacher. The whole group mattered to me, not unlike the way Ramana Maharshi said that the mountain Arunachala was his teacher. I was upset for a few minutes and then intuition let me know that I still had Art.

Sometime towards the end of this phase I had a dream which I knew was significant. I dreamt that my dog and I were walking on a beach when we saw a pack of rats in the distance. There was one very big rat amongst them. He was looking in our direction. I began to get upset as I was afraid of rats and began to call my dog to me so that he would not chase the rats.

Rats for a long time had symbolic meaning in my dreams. As someone who had always paid attention to dreams

129

and particularly the symbolism in dreams I had come to understand that we had two kinds of symbols, universal and personal. This idea, I think, comes from Carl Jung. Because rats had appeared in my dreams over the years, and are rarely mentioned in literature as having universal meaning, I understood that for me they had a specific meaning. They represented that which I feared and rejected in the world.

I have since come to think that rats were the first thing I was taught to fear by my parents. I must have been a very small child when this happened. There was an area near our house where as little kids we were cautioned not to go because it was said there could be rats there. I don't remember ever seeing one. Stories were told about the dangers of rats to children and also where they lived was a dirty area. I suspect that it was then that I developed a fear of them and what they represented. It's only recently I thought about this when I was wondering how symbols get into our psyches. I was aware that what was coming up in my dreams at this stage was from the very depths of the psyche. All my dreams were set in childhood. I suspect that for me rats symbolized my original fears, the root of ego. Self-inquiry and this process had taken me back to the origins of my mind, my ego, the survival program of the organism. This childlike state I found myself to be in might be explained as having lost the layers of rationality and explanations that had covered over this primal fear. With the defenses gone, the primal being was all that was left.

In the dream I was going to turn back to avoid the area where the rat was when something in me said, "No. Keep going on." The rat was looking at us. He looked at us intensely for a moment and then went back to what he was doing. Something said to me, "You can't continue to avoid what you don't like or fear." So, my dog and I continued towards a dirty stagnant stream area where the rats lived and lo and behold, there were a few stepping stones I could use to step over what disgusted me and my dog jumped over. The rats continued with their activity, uninterested in us.

Since rats symbolized what I hated, rejected, feared and found disgusting in the world, the dream showed me that I had finally come to accept what I feared and what disgusted me in the world. Finally, full acceptance of "what is" had arrived. I knew I no longer rejected "what is" and in that realization I could see how so much of my life had circled around resistance to and rejection of situations. Ego is a resistor or a fear machine. Its fundamental thesis is the avoidance of what it deems dangerous, ugly, or unpleasant in the name of survival. And in that rejection much of the joy of life is also thrown out. The inner child is also rejected or quashed. The inner child represents spontaneity, living in the moment, and playing for the simple fun of it.

Also around this time, ego came back, it seemed. Having been living in total equanimity for months, with very little mental activity going on, suddenly mental activity erupted like a volcano. Imagination and fantasizing erupted. The fantasies were all about imagining myself as a spiritual teacher, using every situation to make smart, wise remarks, to promote myself as the wise one, the special one who knew something that nobody else knew. Since I was long since practiced in observing thoughts, I knew this was dangerous. I knew that if I fed these fantasies, started making such remarks to others, it would get a foothold again. But, the sheer intensity of the fantasizing shocked me. There was no emotional aspect to this fantasizing. It was the mind only, relentlessly imagining itself as "The Special One." Since I could look at the mind objectively, this felt like a dying rat in the corner who had been beaten to near death and was suddenly and with great ferocity attacking its attacker back. What I noticed was that these fantasizing spurts couldn't sustain themselves for long. After about a week of these vicious spurts of attack, the fantasizing simply lost its energy. The rat in the corner didn't have the energy to sustain itself for long periods. I could not say it had died, but it didn't have the energy to maintain the attacks for more than five or ten minutes at a time. After the initial round of ferocious attacks it was obvious that it couldn't keep it up, but I was vigilant to not give it a foothold by actually saying any of the "special one" statements. In between spurts, it disappeared, leaving the observer unhindered.

At the time, I thought, this is what is meant by the expression "spiritual ego." The ego tries to capture the spiritual path as its last opportunity to survive. It knows it is under threat and becomes desperate. I considered this a dangerous phase. I was aware that given any opportunity the ego would re-establish itself.

Equanimity was still the default position even during these eruptions of ego activity. The eruptions, while intense, were sporadic and were very obvious when they did arise. There was a profound contrast between the calmness and the ego dominated states. It was like sudden hurricanes erupting on a clear calm day, out of the blue. The contrast between the calm and the storm were all the more obvious for the intensity of the disruption and chaos it created inwardly. I felt that these contrasting states were like a demonstration of how much we suffer from ego. Against the background of calm, this ego disruption was incredibly painful and tortuous. I would have gone through anything to make it stop.

One morning I got out of bed (this was around a month after losing TAT) and as I took a step, leaning my weight on my right foot, I almost lost my balance. It was as if I had been leaning my weight on an invisible cane, and the cane was suddenly collapsed under me. I stumbled and as I did, I knew Art had been taken from me. A wave of tears began to develop and intuition let me know that I would not lose my friendship with Art but that from now on I was on my own. My last prop had been taken from me. This last part of the journey I had to take alone, without any external support. With this came the courage to take on this labor and trust that it would work out alright. It felt just like having reached the point of being ready to go into labor to have a baby. Just as a point comes in physical pregnancy when women just want to get the birth over with, I had come to the point of wanting to have done with ego suffering for good. Even though Universal Mother had not been around for many months, I felt or placed my trust in her taking care of me for this last leg of the journey. I still had no idea how long this phase would last, weeks, months, maybe even years.

The time for the retreat was approaching. I set the house up for someone else to be able to take care of Seamus, dinners left ready, bills paid, emergency numbers left ready and so on. I was leaving on Sunday. On Friday morning, as I put my hand to my head I felt a lump on the left side of my neck. I nearly passed out with shock. It seemed that this lump had developed only very recently, in the past few days, and it had grown so large in a few days that it must be a galloping cancer. I was terri-

133

fied to touch it again, thinking I would find it even bigger than what I had first noticed. I was consumed with terror. The wave of terror passed after about twenty minutes, I'm guessing, and I totally forgot about it for a few hours until something reminded me of it again. In the next wave of terror I tried phoning my doctor to see if I could have an immediate appointment. It was obvious the receptionist heard the terror in my voice, but the doctor had gone on holidays only a few hours earlier. It would be a week before I could see her.

The terror passed and once again equanimity reigned for a few hours. But, another wave of terror arrived and this time I thought of cancelling the solitary retreat and going immediately to the Accident and Emergency unit of the hospital because surely I wouldn't survive the week at the rate this tumor was growing. This state of periods of total terror and irrationality interspersed with periods of total calm and equanimity continued all day Friday. All day Saturday and on Sunday morning, while I was driving to the retreat venue, I had to stop the car a couple of times during the journey because the wave of fear and terror was so intense that I was unable to drive. Then I'd get back in the car and enjoy the beautiful scenery and glorious sunshine until the next wave of terror arose.

During these waves of terror I started to pray to be delivered from these horrendous terrors. I prayed to make it safely to the retreat and to die immediately when I got there. I prayed, "Please, take me; take me now because I can never again go through these terrors." The sincerity of this prayer was complete; it was total helplessness, total admission that I had no control. I was at the mercy of god knows what. This surely must be what John of the Cross described as "the dark night of the soul." However, by the time I arrived at the retreat cabin, the terrors had left. It took a few hours to realize this, and it took a few days before I was confident that they had passed, for now anyway. When I realized that they had passed, I did feel it was a pity that nothing final had happened, as I would now have to go through the terror of facing my death again, or so I thought. But, calmness reigned.

Thus began the last week of Tess's life, with three terror filled days of death, exactly as it had begun with three terror filled days of death when I was around nine years old. I had turned sixty one in July and this was the first week in August 2010. Over fifty years had elapsed from my first horror of death and despite the fact that I would say I had always been aware of death and read everything I could find about it, I had not been able to feel the terror or face it head on for over fifty years. I had somehow succeeded in pushing it away or distracting myself from it. Now, I could no longer avoid it, nor could I turn away from it. It was looming larger than life. It was life. Life and death had become one. And yet, equanimity reigned in this last week living in the face of death.

In the silence of ecstasy self is gone, this time, forever. Initially we do not know this, but wait for its usual return (after ecstasy). When this does not happen, all we know is that "something" is missing. It takes a while to realize self will never return, but with this certitude there is joy, a burden lifted, a lightsomeness, now we can fly! But alas, the moment we try to look inward to the Rider, to our divine Centre ......Oh No! (Bernadette Roberts – Ox Vanishes, Herdsman Remains)

THE FINAL SHIFT OCCURS

8. Ox and Herdsman Vanish

Whip, rope, person, and ox – all merge in No Thing.
This heaven is so vast, no message can stain it.
How may a snowflake exist in a raging fire.
Here are the footprints of the Ancestors.
I have abandoned the whip and ropes

The eighth picture tells us that when the duality of self and reality has been overcome not only is reality (the ox) forgotten, but so is the self (the oxherd); the circle symbolizes the all-encompassing emptiness that constitutes the ground of all things. Now, in the awareness of unceasing transformation and total interconnectedness in every experience one is freed from all craving and hatred for the other. In this freedom there is a sense of the wholeness and perfection of ordinary things. (John Koller)

It is said in spiritual teachings that only when you want Truth as badly as a drowning man wants air is there the conditions for it to happen. This was my condition when I arrived at the retreat cabin. I was shaken to the core by the battle with death and was absolutely determined that I would never again have to go through this, no matter what the cost. I really wanted my life to be over. I longed to be out of this suffering state, at all costs. Nothing could be as bad as or worse than this terror of death. This truly was the dark night, or three dark days, of the soul. And yet, neutrality remained as the default between the waves of terror. These waves of terror are existential angst at its worst. But, instead of more suffering when I got to the cabin, I was met with silence, calm, and peace.

The extreme terror that was experienced was, I'm sure, due to the contrast between it and the equanimity that I had become accustomed to. I had become unable to suppress or minimize emotions so the full fear arose without any ability to minimize it. I was aware that I had not experienced such intense feelings since I had been a child and that the three day terror of death that had hit me as a child had led to the suppression of feelings, and suppression of the thought of death. I had not been able to feel the fear associated with the thought of dying for over fifty years. Sure, I felt twinges of it off and on, but the full intensity had been suppressed. I also think that because of the stability that I had developed I was able to tolerate this terror and not lose my balance or look away from it. It was as if my head was clamped in a vice-grip and I couldn't look anywhere except within. As is said in Dante's Inferno: "Here must all distrust be left behind; all cowardice must be ended." Yes, cowardice had left long before and had been replaced with the determination to face whatever had to be faced head on. It was death, my death that had to be faced, looked into and accepted. In place of cowardice was courage to face whatever had to be faced without any notion of where it might take me. It wasn't even courage; it was full surrender to whatever had taken me this far on this journey. I was fully cognizant that I had no control anyway. It was a matter of trust and faith. "Thy will be done." I truly was "a lamb to the slaughter."

Once I arrived at the retreat place, every time I closed my eyes, there was a show going on inside my head. It was in full Technicolor. Symbolic images and videos arose and passed, slowly. At one stage there was a strong wind blowing outside and I found that sitting with the wind to my left, the inner im-

138

ages blew from left to the right in my head, as if being blo
the wind. Then I turned myself around one hundred and eigh
degrees so that the wind was blowing on my right and the images in my head changed direction as if in response to the wind.
I did this a few times and found it really odd. I wondered about
what's inside and what outside? This is language I had learned
from Douglas Harding as I had been practicing "Seeing" for
years. I thought that the physical barriers, the walls of the cabin
and my skull had become pervious. Inside and outside were
becoming one in me. Over the coming days, there were times
when I didn't know whether my eyes were open or closed and
I often touched them to see which they were. At one level I was
never confused about this but it seemed that my perception was
changing.

At some point I decided to do some "seeing" practice. I
had forgotten about it for a long time. I found I could no longer
"not-see" or make the shift between "seeing" and "not seeing." I
tried to think about what Douglas Harding had said about inside and outside and found I simply could not think about these
things. It seemed irrelevant to even think about these things.
I could only notice them and not even really wonder at them.
My state was that this is "what is"—no explanation or need to
understand what I was experiencing.

Much of the time I couldn't think about anything, so
I simply sat, rested, or walked in the grounds and by the lake,
all the time acutely alert inwardly. It was as if consciousness
was particularly clear, even when the body was tired. Time
vanished. The wind blew. The birds sang. The cows lowed in the
nearby fields. The farmer drove his tractor around. The sound
of distant traffic arose and passed. There was a cat that visited

e or less moved in for the week. He mewed at
hed me when I picked him up. All arose and
ireness.

irnal during the week. On Sunday after army journal: "I feel I can do nothing myself
except to leave ...yself open to Grace." I had brought three
books with me: *The Little Book of Life and Death*, by Douglas
Harding, *The Awareness of Self-Discovery*, by William Samuels
and the third one was *The End of Your World*, by Adyashanti.
The first night I slept for about ten hours and awoke with the
body feeling lethargic but the mind keenly alert. In my journal
I comment about not being able to read or meditate. I spent
many hours staring out at the trees blowing in the wind. For
all the feeling of inner aliveness and clarity, I couldn't focus on
anything for long. I simply stared into space, or into the flames
in the fire, or at the waves on the lake. Staring was the default
setting when the eyes were open.

After a long sleep on Monday night, I commented on
Tuesday that every time I closed my eyes there was something
lurking in the shadows, which I recognized from earlier appearances in dreams. I called it "the black ball of death." I wrote: "I
am now determined to try to catch this black ball of fear. I feel I
have the courage and fearlessness necessary to face this demon.
This must be what's meant by facing your own death." After the
agony of the recent days I was determined to never again have
to go through it—no matter what it took. I was prepared to die,
literally.

That afternoon I commented on the feeling of agita-
tion that had arisen in me along with "feeling the courage and

determination to face whatever." I commented on my eyes going out of focus a lot and wondered if I needed to have them checked when I got home. There is pressure in my head. As I read the section titled Contradistinction in William Samuels' book, *The Awareness of Self-Discovery*, I become acutely aware of the background against which everything arises. Here is a note from my journal from that day: "The act of listening is the field of alert attention—the listening itself is the field of alert spacious still presence."

I made some notes on "Seeing" in relation to contra-distinction, and I tested them in my direct experience. I could clearly distinguish between consciousness and each thing as it arose and passed. Indeed, I was no longer able to not see this distinction. Sitting looking into the fire I began to wonder about awareness being self- aware, consciousness being self-conscious. In my notes I wrote: "Is ego co-opting awareness as an attribute?" Later in these notes I comment that I had spent the last hour playing Klondike on my phone! I gave up trying to figure anything out and went to bed, but not to sleep. I didn't sleep at all that night. The next day, Wednesday, was a strange day, which at the time I put down to the lack of sleep the previous night. This is when the images started appearing every time I closed my tired heavy foggy eyes. I could hardly keep my eyes open that day. At the same time, inside I was acutely alive and vibrant. In my journal, I commented on the sensations between my eyes, behind the bridge of the nose area. An eye looked back at me from this area when I closed my eyes.

In the afternoon I wrote: "Consciousness becomes conscious of itself" and underneath it I wrote: "I am conscious of myself as consciousness." There were more comments about the intensity and variety of images appearing when the eyes were closed and the magnificence of the display of the trees blowing in the wind. Some of the images were threatening and frightening, but I was feeling courageous and determined to face down any threat that arose internally. I felt I was being tested. Several challenges arose in these inner images, always about where did the identification lie, with Tess or Awareness—where did the trust lie. A challenge arose around the nature of my relationship with my children. It was really a question of did I identify with the ego/mother role or as Awareness. I felt challenged to let go of the ego/mother identity in favor of Awareness, and I did so consciously.

I slept reasonably well on Wednesday night. I grappled with the identity issue again on Thursday afternoon. "The perceiver is not Tess. The perceiver is IT perceiving through the body/mind Tess." I didn't sleep again on Thursday night until around 6 am. During the night, the bedroom became filled with spirits/creatures, not evil, but it was as if the room had turned into a rainforest, alive with creatures with open and shut eyes. The experience, while beautiful, was upsetting to the point that I wondered if I was having a mental breakdown and should go home. I decided to continue.

On Friday I awoke feeling drained and unsettled. In the afternoon I walked in the grounds and by the lake. It seemed that all of nature was displaying itself to me in its most glorious form. At one point, silence befell the world, the kind of silence where I could hear everything acutely. This experience had also happened on my previous isolation retreat, nine months earlier. I could hear all the creatures—great and small—eating, competing, reproducing, struggling to survive. Every activ-

ity was about the drive to survive and with that I knew that I was finished with the world. I was finished with the survival struggle. All this activity and struggle was now beyond me. I could struggle no more. The world had lost its hold on me. This was not an emotional thing, simply an irrefutable piece of knowledge—a fact. For me/Tess the world had come to an end.

From this time on every time I closed my eyes there was a spinning star behind the bridge of the nose. It was as if there was an invisible tiny angel drilling a tiny hole in that area. It looked to me like the monstrance used in the Catholic ritual of adoration of the Eucharist (Benediction). However it was a living monstrance as opposed to the solid metal kind I had seen. In one journal entry I commented that there was a gentle rhythmic throbbing on the outside in the spot where the hole was being drilled. I thought this must be what is meant by the opening of the third eye. I was surprised because I had always thought what was referred to as the third eye was higher up on the forehead, where Hindus wear the bindi.

Throughout the week there had been sparkly lights appearing before my eyes, which had made me wonder if there was something going wrong with my brain or eyes. On occasions, it was as if light was emanating from objects. On one occasion my sandals were sitting in the shade beneath a window and they were surrounded by a bright glowing halo. It didn't make sense. That same afternoon there was a post in the porch which glowed so bright that I could hardly see the post itself. I reasoned that the intensity of these experiences was brought on by being on solitary retreat.

One of the days I got what felt like very sudden digestive troubles. It was as if my stomach turned to cement, and I did not know if I was going to vomit or have diarrhea, instantly. Then it suddenly descended into the gut and with three intense waves of pain, it disappeared as suddenly as it arrived. It clearly did not have a physical cause.

Around midnight I was re-reading a part of William Samuel's book and wondering: "How can I not believe thoughts, and still let them run." For a good while now I had been aware of the arising and passing of thoughts, emotions, and everything else, but the thought struck me of how I could live without believing or taking seriously any thoughts. I was wondering if it is possible to live without any beliefs. How could one continue to function without beliefs? It struck me that I had not distinguished between thoughts that arise as part of an immediate daily functioning and thoughts that are generated from a belief. I realized that belief generated thoughts are not necessary but other thoughts simply are. It's a question of being aware of what generates the thought. I was already aware of this but somehow it became clearer or the distinction settled in more deeply, so to speak. I could no longer miss this distinction even at the most subtle level.

Creatures appeared again that night after I got into bed; this time the room was full of embryonic rats, which started to frighten me, knowing that in the blink of an eye the room could be filled with my most feared creature. But, I simply remembered that everything is within Me, as Awareness, and so these creatures were mere objects in the awareness that I am. I saw this as one of the last temptations, a confrontation between ego and Awareness, between "I" and "Me." Ego was still putting up a battle for its existence or authority, using fear as its ploy. At that, they disappeared and I fell into a good sleep.

Saturday morning I awoke rested and relaxed and still wondering if it is possible to not get pulled into thought streams. Throughout the week I had been writing to Art and putting some of what would have been journal entries into a letter to him. My main concern had been spiritual ego, thought streams about how wonderful I am in terms of being spiritually developed. These fantasies played out some scene showing Tess in some glorious light. They were intense when they arose, but they didn't last long. In the light of consciousness the ego generated fantasies could not sustain their impetus for long. But, ego doesn't let go without a good fight.

This morning my question or investigation was how to not get caught up in these fantasies while at the same time allowing them. During the week I had seen the fantasies fighting for attention while at the same time consciousness observed. I was irritated by this intermittent arising of what I knew were foolish fantasies, but that didn't stop them from arising. I was also aware of the dangers of spiritual ego and not wanting to feed it.

From Saturday morning on no more fantasies arose. I didn't have to stop them or let them run. They simply stopped arising. Ego had given up. It could not sustain its fight under the glare of consciousness. It was fighting a losing battle. At one point during the day, I was just looking around when what seemed like a tiny, black, dense marble emanated from between my eyes. I got a fright and had the reaction that one would if a fly or bee suddenly appeared between one's eyes. It came straight out and floated straight into the distance as I watched it fade into the distance. It was only later that I realized that following this experience the drilling behind the eyes had come to an end and then I connected the two experiences.

During this week a number of long forgotten memories appeared and reappeared a few times. They were all from the time of my first marriage. Despite the years of therapy I had undergone, mainly with a view to understanding how that relationship had gone so radically wrong, I still did not understand what had gone wrong. Eventually, I looked at these stray memories, of incidents that happened years apart during the marriage, and saw that there had been a pattern to them. They were events, beyond either of our control which seen as a pattern were all leading to putting a wedge between us. I saw clearly that "life," not either of us, had broken the marriage apart and that we had no control over it. We were but pawns in the game of "Life." Total "letting go" of any subtle resentments that might have remained happened.

By close to midnight, on this last night of the retreat, while sitting looking at the flames of the fire, I was hit three times with the deepest, most sudden blasts of depression I could ever imagine. They hit out of the blue. My mindset was that the retreat was over. I had sealed my letter to Art and I would be getting into bed shortly. In these blasts of depression I suddenly descended into the abyss of despair. Then there was a period, maybe five or ten minutes before the next blast hit. The interval between blasts was totally calm and empty of much thought. I felt as if I had been dipped into the abyss beyond all abysses, the depths of hell. It was beyond anything I could or can describe. They were lightning fast. It was over each time be-

146

fore I could think a thought about it. I had the feeling that this was the extreme point that my system could be taken to without it dying. I knew that this was the fire of transformation, the alchemical process and it was being done in a way that suited this particular organism. The organism was being protected while being subjected to the fires of transformation. I simply sat and observed it. I could say that I endured this transformative process but I did not endure, I had become endurance. Unlike the pangs of labor while giving birth, which I was completely caught up in; with these I observed the pangs while simultaneously undergoing them.

I sat for perhaps another hour or so to see if this process was over. When this dipping into the abyss was finished, it was followed by waves of intense hot flushes. They washed over me like sudden showers of fire. I was used to hot flushes because I was going through menopause, but these three or four waves were of an extraordinary intensity, but uncomfortable as they were, I felt I understood them and so was not disturbed by them in the way the dips into the abyss had surprised and shocked me. At the time I was reminded of childbirth with the waves of intense pain and gaps in between. Like all intense experiences, we don't think about it at the time we are going through it.

So, bags packed and retreat over, I went to bed around midnight, I think. I was sitting in bed. I had just turned the light off and I was checking to see if the curtains were fully drawn, so that I wouldn't be awakened too early in the morning by the sunlight, when IT happened. There was a small light in a corner of the room which I didn't pay much attention to. I was more interested in checking that the curtains on one window were properly closed. Having checked that window, I looked back into the room and saw that this light had come closer and had become bigger. I still ignored it and turned my attention to checking the curtain on the other window. Satisfied that the curtains were fully drawn, I turned my attention back into the room only to find that the light had become very big and was now at my feet at the end of the bed. When I looked at it, it morphed into a tunnel and moved right up in front of my face. This tunnel was filled with amazing pale blue light with entities inside it. The entities beckoned me to join them. I was hesitant but the love or invitation was so compelling that I simply couldn't resist. A gesture of acceptance of the invitation arose in me and with that the tunnel came up over me and absorbed me into itself. The entities disappeared. In this instant everything changed for me. The ox and the herdsman vanished.

Awareness, Silence, No-thingness, The Light, God, The Absolute, pick whichever word you want, was revealed as what I am. I now understand why so many different words are used to describe this; none of them capture it, but they are our best attempts at naming it. This was the moment when everything changed, rather the identification changed. It switched from ego to Awareness and nothing actually changed. I immediately recognized this as if I had always known it, but had forgotten it completely. The bedroom remained the normal bedroom and then Awareness, Me, The Absolute, created a vision at the foot of the bed, arising from Me. This was not by any act of will but an effortless creating, the play of God, you could say. The ephemeral nature of creation was revealed—the joy of creation purely for the joy of creating. The vision showed the outpouring of all creation, and that outpouring emanated from what I am, Awareness. It was incredibly joyful.

Creation comes out of the No-thingness, The Absolute. Everything comes from No-thing. I knew I had found what I had been looking for, for over fifty years. I was not consciously aware that this was what had driven my life except for the last seven years. This is what is going on, always has been, eternally, for everyone. Each of us is the creator of the universe. I know this is not logical or rational, but then again Life doesn't fit into some rational package. Knowing this directly, experientially, removes the need to package it into some rational package. This was experiential knowing, not intellectual. Putting words or thoughts on it came later.

Tess never had been anything but a puppet in creation, an instrument of experience and had become so lost (or identified) in her instrumental role that she had forgotten who she really is. It's not that Tess is an illusion or doesn't matter; it's that this is a limited aspect of who she is. The body and mind are not all that she is and in losing contact with who we are or what we really are, suffering, existential angst arises. In finding the source of all creation, one finds the source of their personal self. All the years of angst had been based on a misidentification and consequent loss of consciousness of our source. I have no memory of what the content of the vision was but the joy of creativity was beyond words. Creation is the great game of Awareness, the great joy, the constant outpouring of Love in and as creation.

When it finished, and I have no idea how long it lasted in relative time terms, I was totally satisfied. I was totally calm and at peace and alive, for the first time in my life. In Christian terms, my soul was satisfied. All my questions had been answered, not one by one or anything like that but the fundamental forgetting and consequent confusion had been removed. I knew what I essentially am and what my relation to creation is. I knew what is eternal about me, and everyone else too. It all made sense now, not intellectually but in my being. This was a homecoming in the deepest sense. What a relief! It felt as if there had been a download of knowledge, but I had no idea what it was. A knowing had happened but I had no idea what that knowing was. I had no words for it and no desire to find words for it. It was a kind of unknowable knowing. There was a fullness in everything and an emptiness in everything simultaneously. I cannot find words to try to describe it any more than this.

The mind was not able to process at this point. In fact, the mind had shut down completely but I did not realize this at the time. I had become the fullness of being. I then turned over and went to sleep for about eight hours.

In one fell swoop the Divine Centre leaves the whole body! God is gone too! The one who dies is not self (it merely slipped away unnoticed, and who cares about it anyway?) rather, it is God who dies. But who can believe such a thing? Unheard of! Considered rationally, of course, it all makes sense; since Ox and Rider were indissolubly One, there cannot be one without the Other. Just as they lived as one, so they die as one. (Bernadette Roberts – Ox and Herdsman Vanished)

Everything is Changed – Nothing is Changed

9. Returning to the Source

Too many steps have been taken
returning to the root and the source.
Better to have been blind and deaf from the beginning!
Dwelling in one's true abode, unconcerned with and without –
The river flows tranquility on and the flowers are red.
I have abandoned the whip and ropes

As the ninth picture shows, when self and reality (as constructs) are left behind, then things are revealed to be just what they are in themselves; streams meander on of themselves and red flowers naturally bloom red. In the ordinary events of life are found the most profound truths. Only by seeking the ox as a separate ultimate reality could the oxherd discover that there is no separate reality; that the ultimate is to be found in the ordinary. (John Koller)

I awoke the next morning, as if an angel who had slept on a cloud. I went to the kitchen to make tea. While waiting for the kettle to boil, something happened. It was as if molecules somewhere far away gathered into a cloud which then turned into a lightning rod and it descended upon me, gentle as a dove and penetrated my head. There was no sense of lightening in this, but I can't think of any other way to describe it. It was gentle, very gentle, but definite. With it came the words "I am Who am" as if all of creation had spoken, gently. With that my mind started up again. I hadn't noticed that my mind was shut down or turned off until it started up again. Words and thoughts began to flow, slowly, with long gaps between the thoughts. The thoughts that arose were all about trying to understand what had happened the night before.

Only recently did I hear Adyashanti speak about an experience he had, the explanation of which he said he came across in his research for his book *Resurrecting Jesus.* In the Gospel of Matthew we read: "So, Jesus comes and is baptized in the water, and at the moment he raises his head the spirit descends into him. As soon as Jesus was baptized, he went up out of the water. At that moment heaven was opened, and he saw the Spirit of God descending like a dove alighting on him" (Matthew 3:16, NIV). This descent of the spirit reorients his whole life, gives his life a new direction. From that instant, Jesus' life is not what it was before. His life became what we read about in the story. I have now come to interpret this experience of the descent of that gentle something into me as being this same experience—the descent of the Holy Spirit, to use Christian terminology.

I knew it was not my mind which said "I Am Who Am" because it was after this that the mind came back into action. I saw it cranking back into action. It was then that I realized that the mind had been shut down for some time. This might explain why I have no memory of the content of the vision. The experience of the night before was beyond the mind and beyond what the mind could conceive so in the process it had shut down.

About an hour after the mind had come back, I (the mind) decided to look inside to see what I was feeling or thinking, only to realize that there was no inside anymore. I was gone, totally. It was then I realized that when there is no inside, there is no outside because inside and outside exist only in relation to each other. There is only This. Consciousness is all, no center, no boundaries. It just is. Despite what I had read or heard about "no self" or "all is one" in the past, the reality of coming upon this was completely unexpected and startling, shocking even. Incidentally, the same thing happened to Seamus, three days before he died, and he had the same reaction. He was startled by the loss of himself. "Seamus is gone," he told me and this was from a man who had not read or heard of these things. Such a thing I could not have imagined. But, here I was and this was the new me—no center, no boundaries—just spacious Awareness. No ego is one thing, no self is another. What I had recognized as ego (the will) had disappeared nine months earlier.

Driving home through the center of Ireland on that glorious sunny Sunday morning following the big change, the mind didn't have much to say about it because the perception of the nothingness in everything and the everythingness in the nothingness was so palpable. I was full of no-thingness and "full" is the important word here—the fullness of being. This something new was everywhere, and I couldn't't turn my attention away from it, not that I wanted to because in the midst of it I found I could function normally and easily. The Buddhist saying "Emptiness is form and form is emptiness" passed through my mind.

I stopped off in a restaurant in a small town and ordered a typical Irish breakfast of bacon and egg. I was hungry. The young waitress who served me, I noticed, couldn't stop looking at me. Even when she was back at her serving station she kept

looking in my direction, as if she couldn't take her eyes off me.
I wondered if there was some outward sign of the change in me
that was obvious to her. I wondered if, when I got home, people
would see a difference in me. They didn't. People said I looked
relaxed after my week away from full time caring and that
was all. I didn't feel like talking about it because I had nothing
to say. I didn't know what to say, but I was surprised that the
change didn't show in some way. How could such a profound
change go unnoticed by those around me? The following day I
asked Seamus if he noticed anything different about me and he
said, "No, did you change your hair style?"

On the way home I mailed my letter to Art, knowing
that it didn't contain the end. I thought I would email him
during the week and let him know, but as the week went on I
couldn't find words to tell him what had happened. All I could
think of writing was "It happened," but I knew he would immediately ask for a description or something, and I was unable
to find any sensible words about it. I felt I should be able to
interpret the experience for him and was unable to do that. As
it happened he got my letter super-fast and emailed me towards
the end of the week asking for further explanation of something
I had written. Then I emailed him and told him, in brief.

Over the following maybe eight or nine months I hardly
slept at all. I slept for about two hours every night but even then
remained aware in some way. Every night I lay in bed, totally
peaceful and watched the mind run around examining all kinds
of experiences and events and trying to understand them. It
was trying to re-interpret memories in light of this new perception. During this time I never felt tired. Eventually, the mind
just gave up, I think, and I began to sleep longer hours. In those

early months, the mind was really out of its depth. It was like a fish swimming in a medium it didn't recognize. It was trying to define a role for itself.

Some weeks into this new way of being, I became aware that I no longer felt even the slightest twinge of fear or anxiety. On looking at this I realized that not only did I no longer experience fear or anxiety, I was incapable of it. Fear had vanished along with the inside. I also became aware of how much people are driven by fear and anxiety and their beliefs and the stories they have constructed to give meaning to their lives. I could see it when I was speaking with people. What's more, I could see that they didn't see this in themselves. I could see egos in action, displaying their hidden roots even though they were covered in social skills and each one's adopted rationale. The individuals were acting out of their stories, in fine detail, but unaware of what they were doing. We are blind to our own egos. This was startlingly obvious to me. I also found that I couldn't read or listen to music or indeed tolerate any unnecessary stimuli. I needed quiet. The seeking was over, so over that I couldn't look at a spiritual book and there were piles of them lying around my house. Gradually, they were put away into shelves. There was a great freedom in this. This was something that I had never thought about before and was a surprising liberation.

There was a great sense of peace and relief, relief that the struggle was over, relief that confusion and insecurity had ended. It felt as if the weight of the world had been lifted from me, a weight I hadn't realized that I was carrying until it was removed. The world, "I," was spacious in a way it had not been before. I was in no doubt that what had happened was the final revelation. I knew I had found what I had been looking for, I

157

knew who I am, but I had no idea of what the implications of this might be for living afterwards. Even though I had known for almost three years that a spiritual pregnancy, so to speak, was taking place in me, I wasn't interested in "motherhood" until the pregnancy had been completed. The spiritual birth had taken place. A new life had dawned. I had given no thought or attention to "what next?"

Very slowly, over the following months, the mind began to find a way to understand what had happened. This was en-abled by remembering statements from the sages and teachers that now were understood for the first time. I felt great gratitude to the teachers who over the millennia had made statements about enlightened being. Before this, such statements had baffled me, now they gave me a language in which to under-stand and articulate what I had become. I tested these state-ments against my own experience of how I now experienced life. Statements such as: to die before you die, the peace that passeth understanding, there is no god outside of you, empti-ness is form and form is emptiness... made sense to me now.

Initially I needed a lot of time alone. Silence drew me back more than anything. I simply couldn't leave it. My daughter got married two months after the change and it was extremely difficult for me to deal with the socialization of the day. Many times I went outside just to have a few moments with Silence. I was exhausted for two days afterwards, not physi-cally exhausted but craving time Alone. I wasn't fit for human company or any such stimuli. Shopping had become painful to me—too much noise, too many colors, too much variety of goods. I wasn't able to focus on mundane matters except at a minimal level. I needed to keep life simple and quiet. At the time I thought I might be like this forever, not really able to function well in the world, but over time I became able to deal with the world again. For the first time I understood why so many on the spiritual path needed the protection of a monastic community. It was for this stage more than the earlier ones. In fact, my life circumstances, being a caregiver to my sick husband did actually give me a kind of monastic life style. The situation relieved me of the need to participate in the world except in a minimal way. I spent all my time either at home or in a hospital without any other demands being made on me. This change truly is being born again and newborns need some protection in order to adapt to their new Being.

Looking back I feel that it wouldn't have helped to have read about this profound change, but in the immediate aftermath of this change I did wish that I had read more about it or that there was someone I could talk to about it. I was unprepared for the sheer enormity of the change, in every aspect of me. I did have email contact with Art but email is a limited form of communication. This is not a condition that can be prepared for by intellectual ideas, any more than knowing about motherhood prepares us for the actuality of it. The reason I had not read about this was that I didn't't understand or couldn't relate to any writings describing it. And, I hadn't expected it to happen to me, despite all the experiences and knowing that there was a spiritual pregnancy going on. Illogical as that sounds, that is how it was with me.

I have since heard phrases such as integration and embodiment for this phase following this realization, and I see that this was what had begun immediately after the experience. This was a period of radical adjustment, of learning to live with the profound shift in perception that had happened. For about two years after the change I had very little to say about it. I was unable to articulate anything comprehensible about it. I remembered incidents, as if disconnected pieces of the path. Gradually these disconnected bits began to join up and I developed something of an overview of the whole journey. Writing this book has been a major step in getting a more comprehensive view of the spiritual journey as it unfolded for me. I can see now that total inner transformation had taken place. I could describe it as an alchemical transformation, say like a lump of brass being transmuted into a lump of gold, still the same shape and same size but changed in essence. And the last couple of years of the journey did feel like there was a fire burning in my soul. While the change was not noticeable externally, internally the landscape had changed totally. It had come to peace. Peace reigned in me.

In his book, *The Rose and The Stone*, Pat Crowley writes "What is unchanging, without beginning or end, however, is the background without which all these appearances could not take place —the pure spirit." The unchanging had come into focus for me and that is a huge shift in one's life. I had to live with this change before I could see what had really changed because ordinary life had remained unchanged. Nothing had changed but everything had changed.

It was probably a year or more when one day I recalled the phrase "being born again," or as Pat Crowley says: "twice born," and realized that this is what has happened. The question was: What had been re-born? Who had been reborn? I had no idea, still don't —because surely, something has remained after the inside disappeared. Experientially I know what I am but trying to articulate it is difficult. Bernadette Roberts, in her book *What is Self?*, looks at this, using Christian language, from the perspective of what is left when self or the inside has gone. She says:

> An entire life's journey of love and trust is now brought to bear on the single unknown moment of permanently crossing the line. The enormous preparation and variety of experiences needed to come to this moment can never be sufficiently stressed. What is meant by the "fine line" between two different dimensions of existence is the difference between a temporary suspension of consciousness (ecstasy) and the irreversible permanent suspension, which is the end of all ecstasy and the beginning of the no-self dimension. In other words, as long as ecstasy is a transient experience, there is always a return to the unitive state, but the moment there is a permanent suspension of self or consciousness, there can be no return. Instead, there begins the adjustment to a totally new dimension of existence, and one that could not have been imagined ahead of time. Ecstasy does not define this new dimension of existence or the no-self condition; rather, ecstasy is only the vehicle or the condition of crossing over to a new dimension of existence. Prior to this moment, ecstasy, as it was experienced during the passage, was only the gauge of readiness for eventually passing over a hitherto unknown line, a line we are not aware of until we are on top of it. The moment consciousness (self) is permanently, irreversibly suspended—with no possibility of return —is a moment unknown to consciousness;

thus the moment of passing over is totally unknown. It is not an 'experience.' Once on the other
side we can no longer speak of ecstasy; there is no
ecstasy anymore because there is no consciousness (self) to be suspended. Here begins a totally
new dimension of existence, one that bears no
comparison to the ecstatic experience. We should
also add that no one—no entity or being, no self
or consciousness—passes over the line. "Passing
over" simply means that all experiences of self or
consciousness have permanently ceased. On the
other side, nothing remains that could possibly
be called a 'self' or 'consciousness.'

This is the best description I have come across concerning what
happened to me.

Christian terminology is not my forte, but I understand
what she is saying and it fits my own experience perfectly. She
uses the words "self" and "consciousness" interchangeably and
I take it that by "ecstasy" she is referring to the many insights,
realizations, experiences, etc., one can have along the way. For
me the final realization was ecstasy, but that was only the actual
experience. That passed and what remains in its wake is a totally
different being. The ordinary has become extraordinary. The
mystery of Being is everywhere to be seen. The extraordinary
is ordinary. This is the simple life experienced without being
filtered through an ego or personal lens. This universal process
or transformation has been experienced by many over the gen-
erations and tracks have been left behind for the new genera-
tion to understand what had happened to them as individuals.
It took about two years before I felt I could articulate anything

about the whole process. I needed to get some distance from the journey before I could get an overview of it. And I needed to live with this change, this new way of experiencing life before I could discern what had changed. It is now almost five years on as I write this, from that fateful night.

Throughout all this time, my husband went through many medical crises, and I was always able to be fully present for him. I got up during the night, did what needed to be done without any resistance to the situation. People began to comment on how calm and steady they found me to be. There was no effort involved in any of this except at a physical level. I did sometimes become tired but somehow the next day an opportunity would arise to catch up on broken sleep. Everything flowed easily and incessantly and continues to. I couldn't help but notice how perfectly everything wove in and out of each other—nothing was/is separate from anything else. It's all one outpouring of creation, pouring out of No-thingness.

Everything emerges from no-thing and falls back into it. The ego fears this No-thingness because it interprets it as nothing. The No-thingness, Awareness, is beyond the perception of the senses and the ego, because ego is that aspect of mind which is the functional tool of the senses. It is the mental tool whose function is to keep the body/organism alive in the world. Awareness is beyond the mind so the mind cannot grasp it. The mind is in Awareness, but it likes to think that Awareness is in it, that it is superior. This is the crux of the problem. The mind claims to be all and as long as we believe the thoughts produced in the mind we are lost in this labyrinth of falsity.

163

Throughout this phase my husband was having regular brushes with death. I saw firsthand his suffering, the anxiety, and the fear associated with identification with the body, thinking that we are the body. The medical system and culture operates on the basis that we are bodies, persons, and once that dies, that is the end. In other words, the assumption is that Awareness resides in the body. The opposite is true; the body is in Awareness, an instrument of experience. But, don't take my word for this. These are merely efforts to articulate that we are more than we think or imagine and only by going through our own journey will we come to know this for ourselves. Taking my word is believing, and we can't believe our way back to our true nature. The assumptions, beliefs, expectations we pick up from society all operate on the basis that we are bodies with associated thoughts and emotions, that we are creatures of the world. Some comfort themselves with the notion that some aspect of the mind or emotions will remain after the body is gone. But, the mind and emotions are necessary associations of the living body and die with the body.

Really, we are not creatures of the world; we are the source of all creation. Being cut off from this knowing is the root of all suffering. The spiritual wisdom of the world, from all traditions, offers us alternative ideas about what we are by way of guidance back to our true Self. Wisdom tries to alert us to our identity as "children of God" as opposed to children of the world. Getting started is not an easy thing for most people because we don't know how to question ourselves. We don't know where to start. So most people, while they may be aware of glitches and contradictions in their thinking or beliefs, decide to turn a blind eye on it because they have not heard that there is a possibility for a final resolution to our predicament hidden in these glitches. There is an assumption that nobody knows what death is, that this is unknowable. Indeed I was shocked when I first came across the notion of "dying before you die." It sounded like an impossible contradiction. I had assumed it meant death of the body whereas in this statement the death referred to is death of the ego or self. As we read in the poem at the beginning of this chapter: "Dwelling in one's true abode, unconcerned with and without – The river flows tranquilly on, and the flowers are red." Yes indeed, the river of consciousness flows tranquilly on when dwelling in our true nature.

For all the talk and writing about "enlightenment" that is currently available in the West, I find that still few people realize that this is a possibility for themselves—that this applies to each one of us, not some special people. It's about taking ourselves seriously enough to examine deeply everything about ourselves. This is where the value of The Perennial Wisdom comes in. The various streams of teachings: Buddhism, Christianity, Islam, Hinduism, all have at their core the notion of a transformation that is possible for everyone. They use different metaphors; they offer different methods for achieving this transformation, but at the core they are talking about the same thing—the hidden potential in the human being. This hidden potential is the possibility of "coming to the end of suffering" as the Buddhist literature says, becoming one with The Christ, as Christianity says, coming to know Consciousness without an object as Hindu literature says. All of them are trying to alert us to the fact that we are no mere human bodies with a mind/emotional dimension. In essence we are Awareness and Awareness doesn't die when one of its instruments dies. But, there

165

isn't much point trying to explain or describe this "condition" because what one is transformed into is indescribable and in-explicable. All I can say is that it is what everyone longs for—to live in peace with ourselves and the world around us.

Taking this potential seriously is The Great Opportunity embedded in being a human. We are no mere animals, although we have an animal dimension. It seems to me that many people are quite content with their human lives and are not interested in this potential or are not driven by desperation to find out about it. But there are others, and I was one of them, who were always disturbed by the superficial explanation of life. I always felt as if I was dancing on The Titanic while the ship was sink-ing. I could never quite forget that death could hit me or those I loved at any time. There was no guarantee in life, no guarantee that I would live to an old age. I saw death striking unexpected-ly all around me. It was this growing desperation that drove me to seeking a solution to my inner discontent. In other words, I became a seeker of spiritual wisdom. Once I made a commit-ted decision to delve into it, I began to come across books and teachings that illuminated the path and teachers who guided the path.

Sometimes this is referred to as The Open Secret, and this is an apt title for it, for when we start to seriously look, we find that others have left tracks behind and we will find oth-ers who are already on this search—the search for Self or God. Radical questions have radical solutions. Despite feeling that there is no solution to our radical questions and doubts, there is. It is to be found in what is commonly known as spiritual seeking.

Beyond this death there is only a Void of Voids – Meister Eckhart's "breakthrough" into the unknowable Essence of the Godhead, The Source, which is God-as-He-is-in-Himself and no longer God-as-He-is-in our-self. This is Meister Eckhart's "barren desert," "the wasteland," "the abyss" of the Godhead. The Essence of the Godhead, however is not fit for a human being, in fact, there is nothing worse in human history than this Void of Voids. Although sensory perception remains, the mind is Void, all form is Void – no God in nature, all creation is an absolute Void. With no experience of life or being, of body or soul, of mind or thought, the only question that can arise is: "What is the true nature of "this" that remains? Obviously, something remains, but the mind has not a single idea. The answer can only be revealed – and so, eventually, it is. (Bernadette Roberts – Returning to the Source)

RETURN TO THE MARKETPLACE

10. Return to the Marketplace

Barefooted and naked of breast,
I mingle with the people of the world.
My clothes are ragged and dust-laden, and I am ever blissful.
I use no magic to extend my life;
Now, before me, the dead trees become alive.
I have abandoned the whip and ropes.

Finally, the tenth picture shows the enlightened oxherd enter-
ing the town marketplace, doing all of the ordinary things that
everyone else does. But because of his deep awareness, everything
he does is quite extraordinary. He does not retreat from the world,
but shares his enlightened existence with everyone around him.
Not only does he lead fishmongers and innkeepers in the way of
the Buddha, but because of his creative energy and the radiance
of his life, even withered trees bloom. (John Koller)

When I look back over my life I can say there were three
streams to it. All three have always been present but
their positions have changed. As a child, family life was the
dominant stream. As a young adult, education, which is the
pre-curser to working life, came on board. As a young woman,
family and work were equally on top with spiritual life as an
underground stream. Over time, the family life stream faded
or became less dominant. At around the same time the career
stream became less powerful. With this, the spiritual stream
came up from underground and with my various efforts it
eventually became the dominant stream. The spiritual stream
had always been present, as it is in everyone, as a small underground stream. Over time it was as if this stream, which had

arisen in the (underground) mountain as a little trickle, became a river and eventually a torrent of water rushed from the high mountain into a lake and eventually came to rest in a still pool, containing the family and career streams within it. Whichever stream we feed, give our attention and energy to, is the one that grows. The spiritual stream arises from a well deep within us. Nowadays, I still, of course, have a family stream, and a little stream of making some money but both these streams flow peacefully in the still pool of who I am.

There is a certain kind of confidence or authority that goes with the final realization, with knowing who we are and who everyone else ultimately is. It's in no way a sense of superiority, feeling better than anyone else, but comes from seeing the big picture of life or existence. Being able to see how we cause our own suffering, unwittingly, and remembering how I too lived like this for almost sixty years is often heartbreaking. I want to show people how to release themselves from these chains. It is poignant and at the same time accompanied by the understanding that as long as another needs to play out their script there is nothing to be done about it.

It's almost five years as I write this since that fateful night in the center of Ireland in a cabin. Nothing has changed and yet everything has changed. I used to hate when I read sentences such as this before the transformation, but now I can find no better way to try to say what has happened to me.

I am often asked what it is like for me now. Let me try to describe it, knowing that anything I write won't really get across what it is like. It is the same as it always was, but without the existential angst, and that makes all the difference in the quality of my life. The capacity for anxiety and stress and fear are gone. There is no legacy of issues from the past. They have disappeared at an emotional level, but I still remember events when in situations that provoke their memory. I am more alive. It's like effortlessly riding the wave of life, occasionally leaning towards heartbreak or joy in the most unexpected moments but quickly recovering and back on the wave.

I am back in the market place.

This transformation isn't an experience although the path leading to it is filled with experiences. Experiences come and go, but once the transformation is complete, that's it. A different "you" remains, the old one having evaporated into nothing. What's left is peace, calm, silence, clarity, in which all the usual relative happenings happen without touching the No-thingness. To use the language of Vedanta, one could say that the distinction between what is consciousness and the constantly arising and passing objects in consciousness is clear. There is no longer any confusion about what one is, although it seems to be impossible to articulate it. One knows what they are experientially, not intellectually. One's identification is always with consciousness as opposed to anything that arises in con-sciousness. Sometimes I say it is like having dual citizenship, in the Absolute and in the person. There is no conflict between the two. One comes to the fore and the other recedes as any situa-tion requires, naturally and effortlessly.

I suffer as much fright as anyone who is almost hit by a bus; adrenaline rushes up through the body and then returns to normal in about a minute, without the need to make a story out of it. It is soon forgotten. Emotions such as this are felt more

intensely than before. There is no capacity to suppress anything that is happening. The suppressor is gone. Excitement is gone or the capacity for excitement. Don't mistake this for a dull condition. It's not. Peace and serenity reign in its place.

The ups and downs of managing daily life remain. My back still bothers me at times, just as it always did. I still smoke, even though I would like to be able to quit the habit. I still drink alcohol on occasions. I think that I look completely normal and ordinary to my friends. Indeed, most of my friends do not know about this aspect of my life and I imagine would be very surprised to hear this about me. And I feel no desire to speak about it unless asked.

Initially I thought I could go on living my quiet private life, but I was outed by a talk I gave to the TAT folk about a year after it happened. The talk was put up on YouTube and there it was; I was out in public as someone who had undergone this transformation, the aim of all spiritual seekers. In order to explain this to my family mainly, I set up a website. That website has attracted seekers and through it I have been able to offer some guidance to those who have contacted me. Surprisingly, I find myself being referred to as a spiritual teacher. I neither hide the fact that this transformation has happened to me nor do I promote it. The website is attracting those who feel drawn to ask me about these matters. I am well aware that not everyone is interested in this, or they already have a path or teaching they are following. I find I cannot resist sharing this journey with anyone who is struggling with their own journey and who asks me about it. How could I not share this information, that the end of suffering is possible for every one and that I know this in my own experience? Perhaps, my speaking out will encourage others to go for it and perhaps my sharing the practices and ideas that helped me along the way will benefit others. This is my motivation for writing this book.

I know that ultimately all ends well, for everyone. Julian of Norwich wrote "All is well and all shall be well." But, in the meantime, in relative terms, the suffering in the world is excruciating. In no way am I immune to the suffering of the world, but I know there is a way out, for everyone. The way out is in submitting to the possibility of a total transmutation. It is nothing short of giving up the notion that we are in control of our lives and submitting to that which creates us—our Source, the source of all creation. This is something each one has to take on for themselves. Each one has to be willing to turn back into themselves, to pay attention to their inner world and experiences and to be willing to examine them in order to see how we are holding on to control, how we are taking credit for things that do not belong to us, and how we unconsciously believe in our own autonomy.

I want to say something about suffering here. In Christian terms it is said "Suffering is the path." This unfortunately is often interpreted to mean that the more I suffer the better or the more spiritual I become. That's not my view of the value of suffering. My view is that we can use our suffering by looking into what causes it, to see how we are contributing to our own suffering, unwittingly. The value of our suffering changes once we realize that it can be used as an aid to our homeward journey. Also, suffering accepted is very different from suffering resisted. The Buddha said, "Life is suffering," It is part and parcel of the human condition. To try to resist it does not alleviate it; it only makes it worse. It takes a change in attitude to go from

173

resistance to acceptance of suffering and this change facilitates our homeward journey. Carl Jung says it this way: "There is no coming to consciousness without pain. People will do anything, no matter how absurd, in order to avoid facing their own soul. One does not become enlightened by imagining figures of light, but by making the darkness conscious. Avoiding ourselves is the key to the continuation of our suffering, both as individuals and as a nation."

When alone, what I think about mostly is ways of sharing something of this path with others. I find the ideas come as a result of speaking with individuals or answering mails about these matters. Like any other activity we do, practice improves it. With spiritual teaching, I am learning with experience what seems to help others and what does not. This is an ongoing process for me. I drink from every wisdom tradition but follow none. This was the path I followed myself so it is what comes to me now. With the arrival of the Internet, we have access to the various wisdom traditions of the world. There is only one thing going on for all human beings, we are trying to find our way back home, back to our original selves. All wisdom traditions are offering maps for this journey.

I find myself repeatedly talking about a few practices and ideas that were beneficial to me on the journey. These include: making the incidents of daily life fodder for your inquiry, learning to become discerning about yourself in every way, becoming self-responsible and self-managing, reading material that will give you a clear idea of where you are, and persevering. Daily life is the spiritual life. They are not separate but streams within the one life. Sometimes people package the "spiritual" aspect of their lives into a weekly visit to church or an hour of meditation in the day or going on retreat every so often. They treat their spiritual life as separate from daily life. This cannot work. Every aspect of us is involved in this transformation. Many, it seems, live out their whole lives at a superficial level. But, others are driven to reflect and question their life. Self-reflection is the doorway into self-inquiry and this means being willing to examine every aspect of our lives. It is what Carl Jung referred to as bringing what is unconscious in us into consciousness.

Becoming discerning about ourselves is about learning to distinguish between different aspects of our inner life. It begins with observation, taking notice of what is actually going on with us as opposed to what we think or would like to be going on for us. Discernment happens at different levels. It requires information to work with because it is the skill of being able to make judgements and accurate assessments between varying aspects of our life. The first stage is becoming aware of patterns within you. Can you see habitual behavioral, emotional, and thought patterns that arise in you? We tend to overlook what is most familiar. We take it for granted.

We need to become discerning in what we read and whose teachings we take seriously. What is the basis for you accepting one teacher over another? Who has credibility in spiritual circles and why? Do you choose a teacher on the basis of their personality or popularity or because they have experienced this transformation and are willing to share it?

Discernment is about knowing what criteria you use to judge every aspect of yourself. This in turn leads to a more focused idea of what you are trying to achieve for yourself. How do you articulate to yourself what it is you are doing? Is your understanding of the goal of spiritual seeking clear and is your understanding of the problem clear? Until you have a clear understanding of your goal and what obstructs this goal, you won't be able to work efficiently and effectively. There are many people who claim to have been on a spiritual quest for decades and seemingly are not making progress. I find that rarely have they a clear idea of what they are doing. In fact, the usual mind-set seems to be one of magical thinking. The assumption is if they keep doing the same thing for a long time it will eventually begin to work. It will magically work one day.

Few have heard that spiritual fruition is a real possibility for them, or else they do not take it seriously. Jesus said: "Knock and the door shall be opened unto you." And, "Seek and you shall find." And he didn't mean, make a light tap on it. Both lack of confidence and lack of intellectual clarity about these ideas interfere with progress. Many seem to think that spirituality does not involve the mind. It's all about feelings and wishful thinking. This is not my experience. It is about clear thinking and effort. This is what discernment is about. Discernment is ultimately about the ability to discriminate between what is relative and what is permanent in us. This happens by a process of seeing the various flickering identities we take on unconsciously in our thoughts and actions, and then seeing one by one, that each one is but a passing attachment. Meanwhile, we become aware of something that is present through all the passing identities. As what is temporary or conditioned thinking and behaviors lose their hold on us, we are automatically becoming more aligned with our true selves.

Self-management, taking full responsibility for the quality of our own lives is an aspect of this journey. This requires discipline, inner discipline. The discipline I am talking about here is about order and direction and focus, as opposed to chaos and randomness and impulsivity. This arises out of discernment, or alternatively supports discernment. The two qualities support each other. Self-management is not just about managing yourself well in your daily life but also about having the discipline to act in accordance with what promotes your main goal, the goal of spiritual fruition. This means not indulging in negative thinking, or fantasizing, and it means having a practice available to direct your attention away from things that are taking your energy and focus and toward your spiritual goal.

Perseverance is also necessary on this path. There are bound to be periods of optimism and depression on this journey. Sometimes, it seems as if we are making progress, and other times it seems that nothing is happening, but if you keep at it, don't lost sight of your goal and keep yourself inspired by reading good material, things will move. This transformation takes place beneath the radar of our usual consciousness. As I said in the book, dreams were what alerted me to seeing that something was happening in me, below mundane consciousness, and they also gave me insights into the progress of the journey for myself. This was helpful.

As I write this, Seamus died a few months ago after a six year battle with leukemia. He died consciously, meaning that he underwent this transformation in the last weeks of his bodily life. About three weeks before the end he was sitting in bed, eyes closed but obviously fully alert and awake inwardly.

He had been mentioning visitations from Our Lady, dreams of great beauty and love and so on, when he said, "Is this what you are always talking about?" I knew he was having some inward visions or the like and when I said "Yes" he simply said, "Oh." His shoulders dropped in relaxation at that moment. He now had a framework in which to make sense of what was happening inside him; he recognized it as the universal process of dying. He had been wary of what I had said about the spiritual journey being one of going through death while still alive and healthy. He told me he didn't understand what I was talking about. But, once he started having inner experiences himself, he understood that this was a known process and that he was not going crazy. He faced into it with courage and trust. Seamus had finally accepted that death was coming soon about three weeks before the end, and during that period he underwent the inner transformation. He didn't find it easy and even on the last day he said to me, "This transition is very hard." He had started using the word "transition" instead of "death" around the last week or ten days before he died. He didn't have any pain so he was not medicated and his mind was clear throughout this journey. Three days before the body died he asked me, "Have you seen Seamus; he's gone." He was startled by this.

What I learned from Seamus was how difficult it is for the ego to give up. "My will" defies and competes with "thy will" down to the last. I don't think any of us can give up by ourselves, only by Grace is that final step taken. The final step is nothing short of acceptance of our personal death, and this, as I found out, turns out to have been the root cause of all my suffering, fear of death. There is ultimately no death. All that dies is the belief that we were a separate something, which is the root cause of all our suffering. With the death of the ego, the death of the belief in ourselves as a separate entity, the identity shifts from the ego to what we really are, Awareness. This shift is not an intellectual understanding. It is much more than that. One's total being undergoes a profound shift. Life after this shift is experienced as peaceful.

This path has no guarantee of success, but, we can, I think, make ourselves "vulnerable to grace," to use an expression I heard from Bart Marshall. Taking the energy we usually invest in ego and investing it intelligently and with determination in non-identification with ego makes us vulnerable to grace. Nowadays, I get mail from seekers, amongst them people who have been for a long time following the Non-dual path. The general pattern I see from them is one of denial of every experience they have, especially the negative ones. They tell me of some event that upset them and then write, "...but I know it didn't happen. It's not real. I know I don't exist." It strikes me that this is a refusal to look deep within them, to take their own experiences seriously, to take themselves seriously. The difficult thing for everyone is to start taking their relationship with themselves seriously, regardless of what teachers or anyone else says. It is sad that such sincere seekers are not getting the idea that we can't bypass ego or simply ditch our suffering but that we have to go through it. Of course, it would be wonderful if we could simply drop it, or wait to win the Enlightenment lottery, but this is a loser's game—magical thinking.

In Christian teachings they talk about two phases of the path: the active phase and the passive phase. The active phase is when we have to do everything we can to promote our own journey. A point comes when the path is taken out of our hands

179

and this is the passive phase. But, you can't bypass the active phase. This is a process of coming home to one's Self, not to somebody else's Self. The way out of suffering is through it, and this means noticing and accepting our every thought, experience, and feeling, action, and so on and examining them to see what the driving force behind them is and where we picked it up. It means undoing our conformity, liberating ourselves from the shackles of conditioned thinking. We have to undo the straightjacket of learned thought we have been packaged into. And we have to start doing this ourselves. After a time it continues to unravel itself.

Richard Rose said "Beyond the mind is a golden find." All the true teachings are trying to point us in the same direction, to find what we are, over and beyond our relative aspect. But we cannot deny or overlook the relative aspect of ourselves. The relative aspect continues as it had prior to the transformation—same personality, same preferences, same circumstances and so on. This journey is not about fixing the ego, personality, circumstances and so on; it is about finding what we truly are, and this includes incorporating our relative aspect into the whole. My experience is that this happens automatically. As I said above, there was a period of adjustment to the different perspective on life.

Back in the marketplace! As I said earlier, it seems nobody around notices the transformation and this is fine. I don't like being the center of attention anyway. I am still in awe of how great some other teachers are at articulating things about this journey, the process and the aftermath to the final realization. I don't see myself as a teacher in the traditional sense, but at the same time I can't stop talking and writing about it. It is the only thing that interests me really. I am sure that this is the most important thing that I can share with the world, in whatever way I can. This book came naturally and easily to me.

When, at the age of sixteen or seventeen, I read Polonius' parting advice to his son Laertes in Shakespeare's play Hamlet, little did I suspect that it would become guidance for how to live for me. With hindsight I can see that the reason for this was that I realized that my religion, Catholicism, was not giving me advice for how to live my life in a way that I could understand, and like a typical teenager, I wasn't willing to listen to my parents. But, I was seeking some guidance for how to behave in the adult world. I took much of the advice in this speech to heart and did live by it, or try to, as best I could. I especially took the last part "This above all," which I always misquoted as "above all else" until I looked it up recently, when deciding on a title for this book. In this last part, his last and most profound advice to his son was, "To thine own self be true." I thought of it simply as "be true to yourself." But, as I soon realized, it wasn't that easy, because I didn't know who or what I was. How could I be true to myself when I didn't know who or what I was really, ultimately, essentially? It was a lifelong koan, which I often brought up in conversations and my reading was directed in an oblique search for ways to become true to myself. With hindsight I can say that this is the search that everyone is on. What is often missed on this search is that we do not become true to ourselves; we become ourselves, we return to the source of our being, and in that becoming, or returning, "And it must follow, as the night the day, Thou canst not then be false to any man."

I see everything with different eyes now. Everyone is "a child of God," on their way back home, whether they are aware of it or not. The troubles I see people going through no longer seem like disasters but God/ Self tearing layers of the ego off that individual—a re-alignment with their True Nature. I very much enjoy the company of my family and friends, alleviated of all sense of judgement that I might have had in the past. I am still perfectly well able to challenge some behavior or statements, but they are never reactions; they are always conscious actions. The great mystery pours out before my eyes, with no idea what will come next. Creation never ceases creating, even if some aspects look very dark from the relative perspective. The big picture changes all. There is poignancy to watching the suffering of others, knowing that they have not yet seen the full implications of what is really happening and always having the "sense" of wanting to put it into a bigger picture for them. I operate on the basis that I am responsible for my actions but I do not own the results—a lesson learned a long time ago on the path. It's not that I think about this, at all; it is just what happens. We are instruments of The Divine.

Awareness, Love, is what we are, not romantic love or anything that the relative or ego can get control of, but truly, all there is, is Love. We are creatures of Love; all creation is the play of Love. What more can I say? It's beyond any words. This "pearl beyond price" is what is at the core of each of us, and it is up to each of us individually to take on the great journey within.

Lo and behold!
Who is this who has risen from the dead?

It is Universal Man, the sum of all creation – Christ!
Now Who, besides Almighty God could have "thunk"
of such a thing, much less made it happen?
"On account of His infinite love He became what we are,
in order that He might make us what He Himself is."
St. Irenaeus (125-202 AD) (Bernadette Roberts – Return to the
Marketplace)

BEFORE ENLIGHTENMENT, CHOP WOOD CARRY WATER,
AFTER ENLIGHTENMENT, CHOP WOOD CARRY WATER.
(ZEN SAYING)

Acknowledgement

I would like to thank Denise Lambert for her invaluable work in editing this book. Her skill and encouragement have taken it from skeletal manuscript to full-bodied book. Thank you Denise.

Thanks also to Bob Fergeson for providing and editing images, rendering them suitable for this work.

Thanks to Miriam Kennedy, Ike Harijanto and Denise Lambert for reading the original manuscript and encouraging me to continue with it.

And last but not least, Art Ticknor for, well... everything.

Appendix: Some Helpful Practices for Spiritual Evolution

Richard Rose advised his students to "leave no stone unturned" in their search for their true nature. Active seeking is necessary and this is the message of all traditional teachings. We have to do our bit in seeking serenity first, even though at a later stage this active seeking is replaced with us being done rather than us being the doers.

What follows are some hints and practices to get you started, or to proceed further. These practices helped me along the way.

Isolation Retreat:

This was a new idea for me when I came across it in TAT. The idea is to spend time alone, for the sole purpose of observing yourself. Since the fundamental aim of spiritual seeking is to "Know Thyself" as it says over the door of the Delphi Oracle, this practice turned out to be one of the most effective practices I took on.

Simply carve out time to spend alone, preferably away from your usual environment as it is often difficult to forget our daily responsibilities when in our usual environment. The idea is to remove as much incoming stimuli as possible, in order to see what is in us (in our psyches) already.

Observe what comes into awareness when there is no one else around, when you don't have to be in communication mode with the world and get a look at what is going on within yourself. It doesn't have to be long periods. 24 hours is a good start. Have you ever spent 24 hours alone for the sole purpose of getting to know yourself? Many people live their whole lives without ever spending time alone, without filling the time with distractions, such as reading, or indulging in some hobby or catching up on unfinished chores.

Modern day life has very little appreciation for spending time alone, for the purpose of getting to know ourselves. The world isn't interested in your relationship with yourself, but this is not a good enough reason for you to not be interested in your relationship with yourself. Take yourself seriously! You don't have to go to a retreat center. Maybe you have a friend who will let you use their house when they are away for a few days or go to a cheap, uninteresting motel overnight. Turn off your phone, the television, the internet, and any other distractions or incoming stimuli.

Bob Fergeson explains it this way:

The practice of the solitary spiritual retreat, or isolation, is a method of self-discovery that has been practiced in one form or another for centuries, from the monks in their quiet cells to the Tibetans in their secluded caves. In today's society with its hurried pace and inescapable technology, this practice of spending time in silence and peace is even more important for those seeking contact with the inner self. If, as Jesus once said, the Kingdom of Heaven is within, we would be well served to begin earnestly looking in that direction.

While books, teachers and the Internet can show us where others have gone before, and give us invaluable contacts, only we ourselves can make the inward journey.

Along with isolation retreats and carving out time alone, I recently gave a talk in which I recommended three activities as practices: prayer, meditation, and contemplation.

Prayer:

Open a conversation between self and Self/God/Absolute/True Self. I have found that there are three stages of prayer:

Vocal Prayer: Speak, write, ask, use the words of other, prayers that speak to your heart, write letters to Self/God/Source/Our Creator and tell her what's on your mind, etc. Read books you find inspiring around the topic of spirituality and try to absorb their message into your daily life. Ask for help, understanding, guidance in your search and notice when some grace is given to you. Self/God often responds by alleviating some situation in your life, or by putting a book, teacher, or friend in your path or by starting some thought streams going. The Self responds in its language, not ours, so learn to hear or notice these responses to your prayers. Express gratitude for the help you are presented with. It doesn't have to be much. Simply noticing that help was offered is enough. Use whatever word or language is most meaningful and natural to you. This is an intimate conversation between you and You.

If you call on God or Self only in times of need it's unlikely that you'll have the inner discernment to recognize the responses to your call. Like all relationships, this is one that needs to be nurtured. This is a totally private matter and like all relationships it takes time to develop and for you to get to know each other.

Befriending Self or God may seem like an old-fashioned idea but I have found that I had been unaware of or dismissed the power of prayer until I started to do it. It's an enriching inner dialogue.

<u>Mental Prayer:</u> Listen, not only with your ears but take notice of graces/gifts that come into your life, have gratitude for what's given, and listen for subtle thoughts, thoughts that do not come from the world or usual thought streams. Have a dialogue with an inspiring book that you read. Absorb the words in the book, as if it is a letter to you from the author.

Mentally list the gifts you take for granted, the simple things in life that are easy for you. Talk to Self throughout the day as if to a best friend and be on the lookout for thoughts that may be a response to some request, for some change, for understanding of an idea or simply for guidance about how to proceed with your efforts at connection.

As prayer develops, we become able to hear inner messages and distinguish them from the usual mental chatter. This was a new and unexpected development for me. One way I recognized it was when I had the idea, out of the blue, you might say, that I should read a book, *The Psychology of the Observer*, by Richard Rose as if it was a personal letter to me from Richard.

Now, that's not a rational idea! He's dead. And he wrote the book for his seeker friends thirty or forty years ago, but I heeded the idea, and I was amazed when indeed this reading amounted to a dialogue, I mean a real, living dialogue between Richard and me, as real and alive and intimate as if he was standing beside me. I couldn't have imagined such a thing, and I recognized the thought streams or responses to my comments and questions that came from Richard as having a particular quality that I had not experienced before.

The difference between vocal and mental prayer is that communication has been established and we recognize it. You recognize the quality of thoughts that come from some other aspect of ourselves or dimension that is new. Some new dimension has developed in us. I came to refer to this new dimension as intuition because it gave me guidance and I knew that this guidance wasn't coming from books or ideas I had heard in the world. There was something specific and intimate about these thought streams that I recognized as important, a new development, and I took it very seriously.

Spiritual Prayer: Let every thought and action be a prayer; Let God/Self share in your daily experiences and dialogue with Self throughout the day whenever you remember. In other words let self and Self be one being, intimate, natural, trusting, best friends, closer than any worldly friend could be. Become of ONE mind.

As the reader may recall, in my experience this intuitive dimension developed as a new "voice"— new thought streams of a different quality arrived. They had a quality of being feminine, Motherly and protective to me. It was a distinctive "voice" and I named it Universal Mother. Others might call it God, their personal god, or maybe a saint they have had devotion to. Whatever, it was new and distinctive and comforting to me,

190

and I took it seriously. This developed into an intimate dialogue between me and UM at first. I became accustomed to this new inner dimension and was greatly comforted by it. I was no longer alone and lost. I had guidance and felt understood and known more that I knew myself. This "voice" or "entity" was a loving, intimate presence within me. This love and intimacy developed to the point where UM and I became one being. What I thought, she thought, what I did, she did. We became I. This was a rich phase on the journey home and I suppose what in Christian terms would be described as a "consolation" or "ecstasy." By the time this dimension came into view I already knew that a "spiritual pregnancy" was afoot in me, even though I had no idea how long it might take to come to fruition.

But the time came when "we" or this new "I" disappeared but that's another part of the path.

Meditation:

Take vacations from the ego, the imposter —the one who is claiming to be the real you but is not.

My way of generalizing what is happening in what are common meditation practices these days is that it is taking a vacation from ego. This is why it feels so good. Ego despite all its promises of making us happy fails. All these failed efforts at finding happiness add to our suffering. To get a break from the obsessive rounds of problems, promises and image maintenance is like a vacation. It's a way of just putting the whole inner show aside for a short period of rest. No wonder so many become addicted to their meditation practices, falsely believing that the more vacations you take the sooner the home problems will disappear or solve themselves in your absence. Having said that, vacations are valuable, if only to learn that there is an alternative way to live or that in getting a vacation from ego we might become able to see it in action. There is a great variety of meditation techniques available nowadays. All have value, I am inclined to think. Go with the one that appeals to you or is easiest for you to practice.

Types of meditation:

Mindfulness: the most well-known practice in the West at the moment. It is often used as a means of dealing with issues in daily life by practicing observing them and not becoming lost in them. It's a version of "being here now" or "being present" throughout the day.

Zazen: sitting for long periods, training in effortlessness.

Transcendental Meditation: repeating a mantra as a means of quieting the mind.

Kundalini: a method of following the breath and using it to move energy up through the body.

Qi gong: Using the breath to circulate energy around the organs of the body.

Trance based practices: using music and other aids to create a state of hypnotic trance, often has euphoric side effects.

Visualization: listening to someone create pleasant scenes into which you imagine yourself.

Heart rhythm meditation: concentrating on the heart region while generating compassionate thoughts about yourself and the world.

Many of these methods of meditation have a relaxing effect, and so become attractive and useful therapies in dealing with daily life. The question is how much or how effective are they helping one find or become their true selves.

Insight/Vipassana: observing thoughts, introspection, observing your inner life in terms of emotions, bodily sensations, thought categories etc. Get to know yourself intimately in your mundane manifestations and thereby come to see the nature of existence, and non-existence.

Seeing: Douglas Harding devised a meditation practice which he refers to as "meditation for the marketplace." In other words you can practice it throughout the day. He offers an alternative view which challenges the authority of the ego: what we have been conditioned to believe. He has written many books. "To Be and not to Be" is a good place to get started with his writing. Check out his website: headlessway.org for more information.

Body scanning: putting attention on body sensations, taking attention away from the mind, the imposter. This can be done throughout the day but usually needs a bit of intensive practice first. Sensations are always in the present tense, and while the attention is trained on the senses, it is off the ego or mind and this inhibits the automatic chatter that goes on. With this practice the ego gradually loses its domineering hold on the attention and the self-feeding mechanism of the ego is interrupted.

Meditation: as described by Art Ticknor:

I meditated over a period of 25 years, admittedly with more discipline in earlier years, before

193

reaching the resolution of the yearning for self-definition that prompted my search. And even after self-realization, I didn't feel like I had any perspective on "What is meditation?" Then, a little more than a year later, a perspective drifted into my mind as I was drifting off to sleep one night.

Meditation is watching.

Like watching squirrels at play? Not exactly. Meditation is watching the mind.

Like watching our thoughts and feelings? That's a step in the right direction. But not exactly it, either. Meditation is watching the watching. How do you do that? By watching the conflict going on in the mind without getting caught up in it. Easier said than done. It requires staying alert to the watching. And then what? The watching will jump to a more interior view within the mind. Like a new eye opening? Not exactly. The more interior watching has been going on while our attention was on a more exterior watching. What will I see? You'll see processes going on within the mind, processes such as decision-making. Like a factory with machinery operating or a computer with programs running. And then what? You'll become aware of the biggest conflict, the main problem that the mind is trying to resolve: What am I? Where did I come from? What's my connection with the world and particularly with this body-mind? Will its death be my end?

Meditation is not drifting off into a pleasant state. There's no state more pleasant than dreamless sleep, and we go there every night, but it doesn't solve the problem. We return to the waking state without a resolution of the yearning for definition. (Substitute your own word or phrase for "definition": meaning, purpose, truth, reality, nirvana, heaven, oneness, love, etc.)

Meditation is reviewing life's traumas, the blows to our self-esteem, and letting them lead our search for the elusive, afflicted and needy self. Meditation is learning to monitor and control or sidestep the physical and mental obstacles to meditation. Meditation is watching until the watcher is known.

The word meditation has taken on a different meaning in the past 50 years, since Eastern gurus came to the West bringing with them practices and methods that were not known or called the same thing in The West. Art told me that Richard Rose's interpretation of meditation was "productive thinking", which is more like what we mean nowadays by self-inquiry or the Christian meaning of Contemplation. It's about using the mind to observe the mind, the mind being the only faculty that is capable of self-observation. Bernadette Roberts describes this as humans having a self-reflective consciousness which is what gives us a sense of self. One part or dimension of the mind can observe another aspect of it.

Seeing the ego in action is one of the most difficult things at the start of this path, so having a method whereby we learn to notice the functioning of our monkey mind is very useful. Seeing it is less painful than being it, but maybe not enough to get to the roots of it.

I have practiced all of the above methods of meditation and gained much for these efforts. Any practice is better than none, I think. One learns inner discipline and learns to prevent the ego from its constant self-feeding while actually doing the practice. What I notice from those who come to me is that often times they have become stuck in using some practice as a therapeutic aid. Interrupting the ego's addictive nature by any practice leads to a more peaceful spell, but it's not enough to uproot the whole structure. As long as the ego or sense of self thinks it's running your life, there is a problem. We have to find what is beyond it for it to lose its hold on us.

Contemplation: (self-inquiry):

This is a program of observing, noticing, categorizing, and questioning every aspect of you, with a view to finding something within yourself which is being overlooked. The goal is to learn to recognize your beliefs, assumptions, expectations, and motivations in your daily actions and reactions. It's about becoming aware of your mental, emotional, and behavior patterns because patterns or habits are unconscious. It's about bringing what is unconscious into consciousness, in order to examine and analyze it, not with a view to improving the personality, but with a view to seeing how your hidden beliefs etc. are causing your suffering. The aim of all spiritual work is to alleviate your suffering by uncovering the hidden roots and checking them for veracity. Most beliefs were unwittingly absorbed as children, with a child's mind, and they do not stand up under mature consideration.

Below are some questions you might ask:

Why do I think.....?

What am I angry, sad, hopeful, hopeless, stressed about? What do I value, value most? and why?

How are my values chosen? Have I picked up my values from those around me or have I chosen my own values? On what basis do I choose one value over another?

What is my greatest fear and what are the assumptions it is based on?

How do I know what I know? — From my own experience, from what someone told me, from my body, intuition?

What am I searching for? What "knowledge" would satisfy my soul? What causes my greatest suffering?

What does the expression "existential angst" mean to me? Can I see it in myself?

Can the world satisfy my soul?

Can I trust my emotions? Do I dismiss my emotions as lesser than thoughts? What value do emotions have to an organism?

What is my fundamental idea about what my life is about? How or where do I start looking within myself?

What kinds of things get my attention? Can I control my attention? What controls my attention?

What do I think is the purpose of spiritual activities? Why do I do what I do?

Am I making progress on my spiritual path? If not, why not? How important is this aspect of my life? Is it an interesting hobby? Am I confident that there can be an end to spiritual seeking for me? What evidence have I got for or against this idea?

What are my ideas about enlightenment, self-realization, moksha?

Is it for special people and who or why are these people special? Am I special and what would be the basis for it?

Bryon Katie's "The Work."

The essence of this method is to confront every issue that arises in your life with four questions.

1. Is it true? (Yes or no. If no, move to 3.)

2. Can you absolutely know that it's true? (Yes or no.)

3. How do you react, what happens, when you believe that thought?

4. Who would you be without the thought?

It is most helpful to generate your own questions, ones that are relevant and meaningful to yourself. Get to know yourself at a subtle level. Watch out for subtle emotions and feelings, the kind of things you might never mention to anyone else but observe in yourself.

Remember, self-inquiry is Experiential.

I am often asked: how exactly does one practice self-inquiry? I think the best way I can explain it is to give an example of how a situation could be used in this way. Let's imagine a situation where you are talking with a friend and the friend makes some casual remark which offends you. It doesn't have to be a big offence; in fact lesser offences make better material for this kind of work, at least for getting started with it. The reason for this is that major offences trigger major emotional reactions, and we get drowned in the emotions for a while. When an offence happens we usually resort to one of two reactions, and reaction is the important word here. The reaction is a triggering of the fight or flight response. We either hit back in some way, usually with some verbal repost, such as humor to distract or we sink into ourselves and withdraw from interaction with the other person. Whichever reaction style we have is a learned method of coping with the interactions of daily life. My teacher Richard Rose used a phrase to describe the less welcome of these interactions: afflictions to the ego. Pretty much all interactions with others either inflate or deflate our sense of self, our ego. The inflating interactions are just as useful in ferreting out our secret motivations and values, but since they are pleasant we are less likely to start with them.

Everyone suffers affliction to their sense of self in daily life and we develop coping mechanisms to deal with it. We try to protect our sense of self, the image we wish to portray to the world. The problem is that we are not conscious of this image. It's an automatic program that is always running when we are in interaction with others. Ego is a verb, not a noun. With self-inquiry, it doesn't matter what our usual reaction is, what matters is to uncover what our reaction is trying to defend. We look to see "what" was offended by the remark of our friend.

Let's say that the friend made a remark that might suggest that I am a mean person, money mean. But, I do not want to be seen as a miser. In fact, I have an image of myself as generous. With self-inquiry I would notice the actual remark, even the word that elicited the emotional reaction in me.

You don't have to act on the emotion and it doesn't matter if you do; what matters is to notice what the actual remark was, not to focus on the reaction. Now, you've caught ego in action. You've seen it in action in your own emotional reaction to the word: mean, miser, thrifty, tight with money, or whatever phrase was used. This alerts you to the fact that you have an underlying belief, assumption, or motivation around this concept. You are offended to be categorized in the category of money-mean people. The image you wish to portray has suffered a blow, probably quite unwittingly by your friend.

We pick up this concept somewhere along the line, most likely in childhood. With self-inquiry the thing is to now take this concept out and look at how it has played out in our life. Have there been other situations where we felt offended by a remark that touched on the same belief? Can we see patterns in our behavior in which we did things to make ourselves look generous or carefree about money?

You might ask yourself: how do I feel about or react to others who seem to be genuinely carefree about money or miserly by my standards? Do I feel others are not appreciative of my generous actions? Do I have little tricks to cover over my mean actions? Having seen this belief or assumption in action, you can now check it out in a more mature way. What are the underlying thoughts behind the money meanness? Do I believe that I have to always look out for my own advantage? Do I feel that others are trying to take advantage of me? Do I feel that I never have enough? What is behind this reaction really? If you stick with the inquiry, over a period of time the real underlying belief will emerge and you'll know it when it shows up.

This is a specialized inquiry, unique to you. The questions you ask and the answers that emerge as true for you may not be true for another. What matters is that you follow your own leads, reactions, and questions that are relevant to you. This truly is an inquiry into the depths of your own psyche. If you see yourself as having been caught out in your money meanness, have you been mean in other ways? Are you a bargain hunter, always looking to get more than it costs you? This applies to relationships and work as much as money. Were you upset that someone saw through you, saw something about you that you had carefully hidden with socialization? Socialization helps us cover up our basic motivations and drives and usually in the process they become hidden from ourselves. The ego by its nature is self-serving, and socialization is the overlying layers we took on to cover it up.

When I use the word ego I am referring to this underlying layer of motivation, beliefs, expectations, values and assumptions that drive our emotions and behavior patterns. The important word here is "underlying" or "hidden". Self-inquiry is the process of uncovering the hidden layers. It's not pleasant work but it is necessary if we want to become true to ourselves and well worth the effort.

This is not an intellectual exercise in that it works only in the midst of your experience. Since you don't know what is hidden, you can't predict what you'll uncover. Self-inquiry is experiential. It's a skill and like all skills it improves with practice. So, it's up to each one of us to uncover the layers of conditioning. No-one else can do this for us. With some understanding of what our goal is, with determination and perseverance and the willingness to use whatever situations are presented, there is bound to be success. My experience was that I was quite quickly able to recognize when I was really getting at the lower layers. From then on it was only a matter of continuing and accepting and dealing with each new find as it happened. It is really quite natural and it leads you along.

One last word, I found I usually couldn't do this inquiry at the moment it arose, because there was another person present, the one who triggered it. You can make a note of what the issue was and do the examination later.

Intuition:

I say intuition took me "Home," back to my true nature. I use the word to mean inner guidance. As you read this you may wonder what I am talking about and so did I for most of my life. With hindsight I can say that I was ignoring it, not giving it credence. One reason for this is that it is not rational and so we cannot defend it to others. In modern Western culture intuition is seen as a lesser faculty, something wishy-washy, suspect even. In our rationally based culture, all things non-rational are underrated or misunderstood. We humans are not just rational beings. There is much more to us. On the contrary intuition is another faculty we humans have. It is our connection with our true selves, and it is always present but if we are in the habit of ignoring it we may not recognize it at first. Encourage the development or more accurately the recognition of intuition in yourself and take it seriously.

Here are a few clues that I came to know in my experience of coming to recognize and value intuition:

Be on the lookout for what in Christian terms is called "the still small voice". This means be on the lookout for subtle thoughts, thoughts that might go by quickly or not be noticed in the midst of all the loud repetitive thought streams that usually dominate our daily minds. Silence and quiet and a calm lifestyle are helpful in this. Lots of distractions, TV, reading etc., keep the mind busy with thoughts coming in from the outside. The more observant you are of the ever changing contents of your mind, the better chance you have of noticing the more subtle fleeting thoughts going through.

You need to develop enough discernment to be able to recognize if the thought is coming from memory, some outside influence or from somewhere unknown. If you don't recognize it as coming from some outside influence or memory, allow for the possibility that it is coming from some inner aspect of yourself. Test it. See if it is worthy of following up on or ask a question about what it might mean. If it is real intuition there will be a follow up.

One way I came to recognize intuitive thoughts is that they were always surprising in some way. It would be something that I would not have thought of myself, so to speak, and often the message suggested a new possibility for something or confirmed something I was wondering about. Intuition tries to get through to us by daily means, the words of a song, what might look like a chance meeting with someone, being given the name of a book or person who has something to show us, coming across something on the internet that grabs our attention. Dreams can be a way intuition gets messages through to us. I recently read a book by Kathleen Duffy, *Awaken to the Wisdom of your Dreams*, which I found to be a very useful way of learning the language of dreams and how to interpret them. I got much value and guidance from my dreams over many years, especially in the later stages of my spiritual path.

Intuition cannot be evoked, only recognized. Like everything in life, the more we pay attention to something in our lives the more it reveals itself. Intuition, like dreams, is specific to the individual and relevant only to the time and place one is in when they come. They are not transferrable which I suppose is another reason the world is not interested in them. Just because the world isn't interested in your inner life is no reason for you to not be interested in it!

One last thing, it is useful to have friends who are also on the path or a group that is inspiring and motivating you to continue on your great journey home.

Works Cited

Adyashanti. *The End of Your World.* Boulder: Sounds True

Angelou, Maya. *Letter to my Daughter.* New York: Random House

Bradshaw, John. *The Family.* Florida: HCI

Browne, Ivor. *Music and Madness.* Ireland: Attic Press

Campbell, Joseph. *The Hero's Journey.* USA: Anchor

Chodron, Pema. *The Places that Scare You, Taking the Leap.* Boston: Shambhala

Duffy, Kathleen. *Awaken to the Wisdom of your Dreams.* Ireland: Covey Publications

Erikson, Erik. *Identity and Life Cycle.* New York: W. W. Norton & Company

Harding, Douglas. *The Hierarchy of Heaven and Earth* and *The Little Book of Life and Death.* UK: The Shollond Trust

Huxley, Aldous. *The Perennial Philosophy.* USA: Harper

Koller, Alice. *An Unknown Woman.* USA: Bantam Books

Krishnamurti, Jiddu. *The First and the Last Freedom.* USA: Harper

Loori, John Daido. *Riding the Ox Home: (Stages on the Path of Enlightenment).* Boston: Shambhala

Merton, Thomas. *New Seeds of Contemplation.* USA: New Directions

Moriarty, John. *Dreamtime.* Ireland: Lilliput Press

Ouspensky, P.D.. *The Fourth Way and In Search of the Miraculous.* London: Vintage

Palmo, Ani Tenzin. *Reflection on a Mountain Lake.* New York: Snow Lion

Rinpoche, Sogyal. *The Tibetan Book of Living and Dying.* San Francisco: Harper

Roberts, Bernadette. *Christian Commentary on the Ten Ox-Herding Pictures.* USA (see bernadettesfriends.blogspot.com for more information.)

Rose, Richard. *Meditation*, and the *Psychology of the Observer.* USA: Rose Publications

Samuels, William. *The Awareness of Self-Discovery.* USA: Butterfly Publishing House

Segal, Suzanne. *Collision with the Infinite.* USA: Blue Dove Press

Sheehy, Gail. *Passages.* USA: Ballantine Books

Teresa of Avila. *The Interior Castle.* UK: Penguin Classics

Tweedie, Irina. *The Chasm of Fire.* UK: The Golden Sufi Centre

Tzu, Lao. *The Tao Te Ching, Jonathan's Star's translation.* USA: Tarcher

Additional TAT Press Books

A Handyman's Common Sense Guide to Spiritual Seeking. An Army veteran, surveyor, reporter, and jack-of-all-trades handyman offers an unwavering portrait of the determination and single-mindedness that led him to experience what he calls completion. Alternating between practical advice and heartfelt exhortations, he inspires readers to pursue their own understanding of existence. ISBN: 9780979963087.

 *At Home with the Inner Self.* Jim Burns was the only living person that Richard Rose spoke of as having "made the trip." *At Home with the Inner Self* consists of transcripts from informal talks recorded in 1984 and 1985. New to the third edition is an interview conducted in 2006 as well as the photographs that evoke the graceful dissolution of the urban landscape that Jim calls home. ISBN: 9780979963070.

Beyond Mind, Beyond Death. An anthology of the best essays, poems, and humor from the TAT Forum online magazine. Many are the voices in this volume, from classic to contemporary, yet all point toward a greater reality than that of which we are typically aware—a Reality that can only be hinted at with words; that must and can be discovered by you rather than described by an author. ISBN: 9780979963001.

 *The Celibate Seeker: An Exploration of Celibacy as a Modern Spiritual Practice* by Shawn Nevins. A survey of people's experiences with celibacy as a spiritual practice. Examines the effect of celibacy on intuition and energy level as well as other benefits and difficulties of this practice. Offers a wealth of practical advice and insight. ISBN: 9780979963032.

The Listening Attention by Bob Fergeson. How can we re-connect, open the Gateway to Within, and once more gain the Peace and Understanding of our Inner Self? The Listening Attention is our innate ability to observe the world and ourselves without identification. Separate from the world of the mind and action, it points the way home. ISBN: 9780979963063.

The Perennial Way by Bart Marshall. New English versions of Yoga Sutras, Dhammapada, Heart Sutra, Ashtavakra Gita, Faith Mind Sutra, and Tao Te Ching. These insightful new versions are presented without commentary ... clear and poetic, yet intensely faithful to the language and nuance of the originals, they invite direct communication with the masters, and vibrate with a revelatory self-evidence that resonates in the mind and heart long after reading. ISBN: 9780979963049.

Solid Ground of Being. In sharing the simple facts of his life experience, Art Ticknor takes us on an extraordinary journey, which hopes "to inspire another with a possibly unimagined possibility, and to encourage another to persevere." ISBN: 9780979963056.

Beyond Relativity. Ticknor's work is a beautiful story of despair and hope: a family man with a fine life and a gnawing emptiness of meaning, who finds himself on a wild ride of a spiritual path. Ticknor shares his lessons and discoveries - from human failings to transcendent revelations with an insider's view of what it means to be a modern spiritual seeker. ISBN: 9780979963094.

Images of Essence. Shawn Nevins and Bob Fergeson team up to produce a gorgeous book of photographs and poetry that embrace the Now. Their work has been hailed as like "Rumi with a Nikon." ISBN: 978-0986445705.

These books are available at Amazon.com and other booksellers. See the TAT Foundation website at www.tatfoundation.org for books, audio files and DVDs published by TAT.

Pat Cronly The Rose & The Stone
Douglas Harding – "To be & not to be" 193
Richard Rose – The Psychology of the Observer 189
Awaken to The Wisdom of Your Dream
    Kathleen Duffy 204

Made in the USA
Las Vegas, NV
23 November 2021